THE DAO OF BEING JEWISH AND OTHER STORIES

*Seeking Jewish Narrative
All Over the World*

IRENE SHALAND

DEDICATION

To my family with love: Alex and Michelle, you are
my life and my light.

CONTENTS

ACKNOWLEDGMENTS

This book grew out of my travels and conversations. I owe a debt of gratitude to many people who helped and supported me throughout the entire project.

My husband Alex is my best friend and soulmate, travel partner, and photographer: without his inspiration, encouragement, and unwavering support, this book would have never been written and without his photographs, it would be mute. Our daughter Michelle, an editor par excellence, applied her expertise and superb sense of language to every story in this book.

My warmest thanks go to my life-long friends, Sandra Kramer, Sophia Muchnik, and Kelly Sheppard, all passionate history and literature-lovers, who dedicated their time to reading my entire manuscript and offering their invaluable comments. Larisa Baumberg's artistic talent and expert assistance with the cover design was vital for bringing my book to life.

I am deeply grateful to my cousin and friend, Hanoch Ben-Yami, Professor and Head of Philosophy at the Central European University of Budapest, Hungary. His visit to Vileyka inspired me to write the Holocaust narrative of our family. With respect and admiration for her courage in sharing her mother's heart-wrenching story of survival, I am thankful to my friend Rachel Matthews (Raya). My heartfelt thanks go to Barbara Aiello, the first liberal Rabbi in Italy, and Bianca Del Bello, my friend and contributor to the chapter on Palermo, whose insights and stories helped me to understand the Anousim of the South of Italy and the inspirational Jewish Renaissance movement. My friend Barbara Steenstrup, Vice Chairperson of the Nairobi Hebrew Congregation and publisher of the Shelanu Magazine, was my patient guide to Jewish history in Africa.

My thankful appreciation goes to Usha and Raj Ahmed, founders and owners of the renowned Chicago-based company Exotic Journeys, Inc., whose organizational talent, endless patience, and extensive knowledge of Asia and Africa made our explorations of those regions possible. Without them, none of my fascinating personal encounters and conversations in India, China, and Kenya would have taken place.

I want to thank the United States Holocaust Museum's curatorial and archival staff who helped to find and select photographs essential for this book, and allowed me to use them.*

My friends Alla Abrukin of New York, Bianca Del Bello, and Giuliana Torre, both of Palermo, and Anoop Yadav of Delhi had graciously offered their photographs without which my stories about the Holocaust, Palermo, and Delhi would not be complete.

Finally, I am forever in debt to the wonderful people from many countries that met with me, offered their thoughts and insight, and answered my endless questions. Here they are:

China: Mike Jing, Director of Operations for the Chinese Government Tourist Authority.
Denmark: Oren Atzmor, Chief Cantor of the Great Synagogue of Copenhagen.
India: Ezekiel Isaac Malekar, Delhi Jewish Community leader, Rabbi, Cantor, attorney, and author of numerous publications dealing with Jewish identity in India.
Norway: Sidsel Levin, Director of the Jewish Museum; Ann Elizabeth Mellbye, Deputy Head of Administration of the Center for Studies of Holocaust and Religious Minorities; and Lior Habash, architecture student—all from Oslo.
Sweden: John Gradowski, Head of Information and Public Relations for the Jewish Community of Stockholm and Ira Vlasova, guide at Stockholm City Hall.
Siracusa, Sicily: Rabbi Stefano di Mauro, MD, PhD, first Rabbi and founder of the first modern synagogue.

All of the above individuals made the stories in this book a proud testimony to the eternal spirit of the Jewish people.

*The United States Holocaust Memorial Museum's disclaimer: "The views or opinions expressed in this book do not necessarily reflect the views or policy of the United States Holocaust Memorial Museum."

FOREWORD

L'Dor Va'Dor

About six years ago, my husband Alex and I were participating in Yom Kippur services in our temple, singing the all-familiar *"L'Dor Va'Dor"* (From Generation to Generation). And suddenly something happened. These words, ubiquitous in Jewish life, found everywhere from bar mitzvah invitations to donor walls, sounded to me like a call to action. "We are words and we are stories…We are carriers of wisdom…Not the first and not the last…" The congregation was singing *"La'Dor Va'Dor nagid godlecha,"* and I knew then and there that I would write this book.

Alex and I have a life-long passion for travel with a higher purpose. Together we have visited over sixty countries. We see travel as a process of growth, a personal art form that we—never as tourists, but always as students—create out of our memories and feelings, the places we visit, and people we meet. Globe-trotting, we make friends, create photo-galleries and slide shows, and write articles and lectures. Six years ago, on that Yom Kippur morning, I made a decision to re-focus our travel on collecting Jewish narratives. Because we are the stories we tell to ourselves, to others, and to the world.

Monument Against War and Fascism in Vienna. An elderly Jewish
man forced to scrub the streets commemorates the Jewish victims.

CHAPTER 1: AUSTRIA

Stones Fill the Void:
Visiting the Murdered Jews of Vienna

"…memory is the keyword, which combines past and present, past and future…"
Elie Wiesel

The starting point of our journey is paradoxically a no entry land, which for me, for most of my adult life, was Vienna. My husband and I, world travelers and art lovers, could describe every Titian and Bruegel in the Viennese Kunsthistorische Museum and the location of every Klimt in the city, but for a long time an invisible barrier stopped us from visiting the real Vienna. At the center of my mental Vienna, the embodiment of refinement and sophistication, there was the image of a 1938 photograph I saw in the United States Holocaust Museum. It depicted an elderly Jewish man, bearded and bespectacled, crouching in the street and scrubbing the pavement with a brush. The crowd around him, jeering and laughing, formed a tight inescapable ring.

In 2010, when we began collecting Jewish stories for this book, the time had come for us to visit Vienna, see the present, remember the past, and imagine the unimaginable.

On a sunny April day in 2010, we found ourselves in the city of the dead. Surrounded by noise of the big city—cars speeding, trams clunking, people hurrying about their mid-day business—we were talking to ghosts, some 65,000 of them, the murdered Jews of Austria. We had come to Leopoldstadt, Vienna's Second District, to follow the *Steinedererinnerung* or Stones of Remembrance. These are brass plaques, 3 ¾ by 3 ¾ inches, placed either on buildings or embedded in the pavement, often in blocks of four, often with an adjacent explanation plaque, and always with names. Each name is accompanied by a date of birth and a date of deportation. One explanation plaque reads: "For the many people who were murdered and whom nobody remembers."

Without remembrance, Italian author and Auschwitz survivor Primo Levy says, there is no future. In Leopoldstadt, the victims are remembered. They have their names back. They talk to us once again because the stones fill the void. All we have to do is to follow their path and listen to their stories.

The "Jewish Question" in Vienna

Don't look for the Steinedererinnerung in your guidebook: the murdered Jews of Austria have neither a Rick Steves nor a Frommer. And Vienna, basking in its Baroque and Art Nouveau splendor, would rather have you waltzing from Schonbrunn palace to Sachertorte's shops instead of searching out the synagogues and homes of long-gone Jews. An Austrian sarcastic proverb, as noted by Magrit Reiter in her conference presentation "Antisemitism in Austria after the Shoa," declares that Germans were the "better Nazis," while Austrians were definitely the "better anti-Semites."

The Holocaust victims' destiny was, for the most part, determined by three key factors: the degree of control the Nazis had in the region, the history of Jews there, and the actions of the locals. The latter is where the Viennese truly excelled. Austrian inventiveness and viciousness quickly turned the city of Mahler and Freud into the city of "Hitler's willing executioners," using the title of the famous book written by Daniel Goldhagen. In this controversial study, Goldhagen argued that virulent "eliminationist antisemitism" was the cornerstone of German national identity. Austrians, in their zeal to eliminate their Jewish countrymen, managed to surprise even the Germans.

Vienna was by no means the only European city where the "final solution" had been successfully carried out. However, the delight the Viennese took in humiliating, torturing, and killing their Jewish neighbors was truly extraordinary. In that 1938 photograph I mentioned, the people in the laughing crowd taking such a delight in humiliating a Jew, were the very ones (or their parents) who elected the rabidly anti-Semitic Karl Lueger as a mayor of Vienna five times between 1897 and 1910. Hitler adored Lueger and considered the Viennese mayor to be a major influence on shaping his views on race.

According to the Austrian Jewish Community statistics, in 1938, 206,000 persons of Jewish decent had been living in the Austrian capital; one out of ten Viennese residents was Jewish. Less than 2,000 survived the camps. Practically no one returned. The flourishing Jewish community of Austria was all but obliterated during World War II. At first, Austrian Jews were lucky: unlike Germany, Austria had exit avenues open for a while and almost two thirds of the country's Jews left. Those who stayed died wretched deaths at places like Theresienstadt and Auschwitz. One Vienna resident, Sigmund Freud, went to London with his family; his two elderly sisters stayed and perished.

After the war, Austria's official position was that the country had been the very first victim of the Nazis' aggression. Austria had no Nuremberg-like trials for crimes against humanity, and this fictional claim went unchallenged for many decades.

Exploring Jewish Vienna today

The rebuilt Jewish community of Vienna is small and for the most part consists of Eastern European immigrants. Austrian officials were not interested in inviting survivors to return. Their shops and businesses had changed owners, university chairs and medical practices had been taken and, as some admit today, many Vienna apartments still have furniture and art objects "borrowed" from Jewish neighbors. So why bother?

And the Austrians did not, until July of 1991, when the Austrian government issued a statement acknowledging that Austria had taken part in the atrocities committed by the Nazis. To showcase its regret, the government even reconstructed a synagogue in Innsbruck (1993) and the Jewish Library in Vienna (1994): both had been burned in 1938. Unlike Germany, which continues its journey of consciousness into the painful past, Austria's half-hearted efforts of reconciling its historic accounts continue to overshadow the Jewish history a visitor might want to explore.

If you follow the established tourist route of Jewish Vienna, you will most probably start with the Monument Against War and Fascism at Albertinaplatz. The monument's four free-standing sculptures are meant to be thought-provoking, but their symbolism is difficult to decipher. One statue, with its head buried in the stone, is a metaphor of either entering the underworld, like Orpheus, or of hiding away from reality. Another is a declaration of human rights etched in stone. The split sculpture, called the Gates of Violence, is dedicated to all victims of violence. The murdered Jews of Austria are commemorated by a bulky, hunched-over figure, which, as you might see when you hunch over it, is a bearded man with a brush. A piece of barbed wire stretched across his back is not meant to remind you of extermination camps: it is to warn you or your dog against using this kneeling Jew as a bench or toilet.

Even when I found out that this monument was literally built on top of human bones—beneath it is a cellar used as a bomb shelter where everyone was killed during the Allied bombing—its emotional impact was still lost on me.

The tourist's exploration of Jewish Vienna usually continues to the Judisches Museum in the Palais Eskeles, near the Mozarthaus. Founded in 1896, it is the oldest institution of its kind in the world. Closed in 1938, the Judisches Museum did not reopen until 1989.

The museum is housed in the former mansion built and owned by Baron Bernhard von Eskeles (1753-1839), a Viennese Jew. A personification of Jewish Vienna at the time of the Enlightenment, Baron was the son of the renowned Polish-Moravian Rabbi. He became a co-founder of an international banking house and a financial advisor to three emperors, Joseph II, Francis I, and Francis II. A patron of Mozart, Eskeles also hosted politicians like Talleyrand and Wellington in his house. The Judisches Museum is dedicated to the highly-important contributions the Jews of Vienna made to Austria's economics, arts, science, medicine, philosophy, politics, and music. "Remove the Jews from Vienna's history," wrote Hellmut Andics in his book The Jews in Vienna, "and what is left is a torso."

The museum's Max Berger Judaica collection is certainly worth seeing, as is the museum's take on history through multiple holograms that provide insights and comments. The museum's intent is not to focus on the tragic end of this brilliant community during the Holocaust. However, if you work your way up to the top floor's viewable storage area, you will see objects, scorched by fire and broken, with some showing the footprint of a boot. These objects were brutally torn from synagogues and households—all destroyed in 1938.

The Judisches Museum has a partner, the Museum Judenplatz. A faceless modern building with bunker style narrow corridors, this museum exhibits the excavated ruins of the city's 13th-century synagogue and focuses on medieval Jewry. Opened in 2000, on one of the most charming squares in today's central Vienna, the museum is situated where a medieval Jewish ghetto used to be. There, the first Jewish community of Vienna, regarded as the leading and most learned among German-speaking Jewry, was annihilated: burned at the stake, tortured, and expelled. Those who barricaded themselves and their families in the synagogue were burned alive. The year was 1421 and the Archduke of Austria Albert V needed money. And what was a "better" way to fill the coffers than to take the money from the Jews and then kill or expel them? A 15th-century plaque mentions this "great pogrom."

The Jews murdered in the 20th century are also commemorated on Judenplatz by the first and only Holocaust Memorial in Austria. Inaugurated the same year as the Museum Judenplatz, the memorial was designed by (non-Jewish) British artist Rachel Whiteread and is a reinforced concrete cube that symbolizes a dead library: the doors are locked and the walls are formed by books with spines facing inward, so one cannot read the book's title or author's name. Around the memorial's base are the names of the concentration camps to which the 65,000 Jews were deported.

As I stood there, the memory of another memorial, the memorial to the Murdered Jews of Europe in Berlin, came to mind. There, hundreds of black concrete slabs, varying in height on a sloping field, create the uneasy, troubling experience of going through a surreal necropolis that had lost touch with humanity: European civilization turned into a cemetery. Facing the concrete cube in Vienna, I understood the idea behind the "dead" library—the books cannot be read because the People of the Book are dead—but I did not feel the emotional impact I had experienced in Berlin. A statue of Gotthold Lessing, the 18th-century writer and philosopher, stands nearby, as an ironic reminder of the enlightenment and humanism of Germanic culture.

From the Judenplatz one can follow the Seitenstettngasse to the Stadttempel, the only Viennese synagogue not destroyed during Kristallnacht. The reason it still stands goes back to the year 1781. In that year, Emperor Joseph II issued his Edict of Tolerance. The edict allowed Jews to build synagogues in Vienna, but the synagogue building could not be a free-standing structure, could not look like a synagogue, and could not have the entrance on a main thoroughfare. So in November of 1938, the Nazis did not burn the Stadttempel out of fear that the entire block where many of the prominent fascists lived would go up in flames. In 2002, the Stadttempel unveiled its own memorial with victims' names engraved on rotating slate tablets.

Across the river

To truly experience the victims' stories you have to leave Judenplatz, where no Jew has lived since the 15th century, and go across the river to Leopoldstadt. In this Viennese suburb, Theodor Herzl lived, Sigmund Freud spent his youth, and composers Arnold Schonberg and Oscar Strauss were born. Leopoldstadt was a Central European stronghold of Zionism and Chassidism where Viennese Jewry created a vibrant, cultured life. The Nazis turned it into a ghetto from where the Jews of Austria were sent to concentration camps and death.

In today's Leopoldstadt, their lives, culture, and suffering are recognized, acknowledged, and made visible through the efforts of the Path of Remembrance Society, founded by Dr. Elizabeth Ben David-Hindler in 2006. Throughout the neighborhood the Society placed brass plaques called the Stones of Remembrance that contain information about Jewish institutions, organizations, and individuals who were victims of the Holocaust.

Dr. Ben David-Hindler, the chairwoman of the Society said: "Our wish is to keep alive…the memory of Jewish life…as well as to give back—symbolically—a place in the home city to those who were expelled and murdered." Dr. Ben David-Hindler's initiative was inspired by the *Stolpersteine* (stumbling stones), a project originated in Germany by artist Gunter Demnig to commemorate the individuals deported and killed by the Nazis. The uniqueness of Dr. Ben David-Hidler's initiative is that it endeavors to not only commemorate the victims but also to eternalize the vibrant cultural life they created.

With a map sent by the Society, you can follow the Path of Remembrance. Most people begin at the place where Leopoldstadt Synagogue once stood and then stroll through the neighborhood's streets searching for places where Jewish theaters, charity organizations, social clubs, and coffee houses—the world of Jewish intellectuals and artists, shopkeepers, and politicians—once existed.

In the middle of busy Nestroyplatz, a plaque commemorates Bernard and Adele Sachs. The building they once lived in no longer exists, but they were passionate theater lovers and they used to cross the square on their frequent trips to the theater. Kurt Sachs, their surviving son, placed the plaque where he knew his parents walked often, happy and young and full of life.

The Society's hope, as noted by Dr. Ben David-Hindler, is "to contribute to the healing of a deep wound."

The Path of Remembrance is the only true memorial that attempts to bring closure to the painful memories of the Holocaust in Austria.

Selected Sources

Andics, H. The Jews in Vienna. Kreymayr & Scheriar, 1988.

Goldhagen, D. Hitler's Willing Executioners: Ordinary Germans and the Holocaust. Knoph, 1996.

Reiter, M. "Antisemitism in Austria after the Shoa." Presentation at Antisemitism in Europe Today, International Conference, Berlin, November 8-9, 2013.

Silverman, L. Becoming Austrians: Jews and Culture between the World Wars. Oxford University Press, Reprint Edition, 2015.

The Path of Remembrance Society's website: http://www.steinedererinnerung.net

Viennese Jews scrubbing the streets. Courtesy of the United States Holocaust Memorial Museum.

Happy Viennese welcome the Nazis. Courtesy of the United States Holocaust Memorial Museum.

Monument Against War and Fascism in Vienna. Orpheus entering the underworld and the stela with Declaration of Human Rights.

Judisches Museum in Vienna. Jewish religious objects scorched by fire during Kristallnacht.

Museum Judenplatz in Vienna displays the excavated ruins of the synagogue burned in 1421 on the orders of the Archduke of Austria.

Vienna Holocaust Memorial on Judenplatz symbolizes a dead library. The doors are locked and the books face inwards.

Staatstempl is the only synagogue in Vienna not destroyed during Kristallnacht.

The Path of Remembrance in Leopoldstadt. The plaques commemorate "many people who were murdered and whom nobody remembers."

"Kafka" in Prague: this curious Old Town statue embodies the strangeness of the "Kafkaesque" world. It also makes you smile.

CHAPTER 2: CZECH REPUBLIC

Seeking Kafka in Prague

"Prague won't let us go...This little mother has claws..." Franz Kafka in a letter to his friend Oskar Pollack.

"And yet – Kafka was Prague and Prague was Kafka...And we his friends...knew that Prague permeated all of Kafka's writings in the most refined minuscule quantities..." Jonannes Urzidil in There Goes Kafka.

After following the Path of Remembrance in Vienna's Leopoldstadt, Alex and I felt drained and emotionally unable to return to central Vienna. All we wanted at that point was to leave Austria behind. Our minds required an intellectual diversion. For some reason, we began talking about Franz Kafka (1883-1924), our much beloved writer, and how lucky he was to die from tuberculosis almost a decade prior to Hitler's coming to power. Kafka was an archetypal intellectual of the Austro-Hungarian Empire in the beginning of the twentieth century. A Prague Jew, whose identification with his Jewish heritage was very complex, Kafka considered German his native language. His haunting stories are filled with bizarre twists of fate—a hostile universe of suffering and alienation. Unknown in his lifetime, Kafka became one of the greatest and most influential European writers after the Second World War.

We were seeking Kafka, and his Prague was our next destination.

Forty years in the making

We arrived in Prague in mid-April, yet it felt more like November: cold, gray, rainy, gloomy, and strangely, emotionally familiar. I had two books in my backpack: *The Complete Stories of Franz Kafka* and his

Letters to Friends, Family and Editors. "Here we are," I patted my book bag. "After almost forty years, we are in the city you loved to hate."

My husband and I each discovered Franz Kafka in the seventies while still in high school in the Soviet Union. We were swept away and overwhelmed by the turbulence of his stories and had often wondered why Kafka was ever translated in the bleak and depressing world of Brezhnev's U.S.S.R. Everything we read in Kafka was about uncertainty and loneliness, futility and repeated failures. His was a world of oppressive reality and bizarre life changes. That world was filled with endless struggle with authority and bureaucracy. And it was a world each of us knew. The literary term "Kafkaesque" seemed to best describe our life in the Soviet Union: hopeless situations, bitter, ironic twists of fate, alienation, and nihilism.

However, unlike the characters in Kafka's stories—and luckily for us—we were able to leave that world behind. When the Communist dictatorship in the entire Eastern Bloc came to an end, the road to Prague—the city that permeated every page of Kafka's books—was open and we, readers of Kafka for almost four decades, became empowered to discover his city. But, as we found, to step into the Prague of Kafka (1883-1924) you have to immerse yourself first in the author's imagination.

The challenge for a Kafka literary pilgrim

There was Kafka in Prague and there is Prague in Kafka—two different entities to understand and navigate. You find very little of what might be called "Prague prose" in Kafka's writing. With the exception of his early story, *Description of a Struggle*, Kafka never mentioned his native city as a specific place, and there are no direct descriptions of Prague settings in his prose. You find, instead, remarkably transformed and dispersed fragments of reality in the strangest of contexts. Prague, in its peculiar indirect and unobtrusive way, is forever present in Kafka's work.

Prague influenced everything Kafka was as an artist and a man. In his diaries and letters, he never stopped talking about Prague: the eccentric charm of its medieval streets and the city's peculiar legends. Prague was where Kafka felt condemned to suffer an insecure and futile existence. In his many letters, the city became increasingly associated with his anxieties. "I cannot live in Prague...I do not know if I can live anywhere else. But that I cannot live here—that is the least doubtful thing I know," he wrote in 1919 in the *Letter to His Father*.

How would we, as Kafka pilgrims, even attempt to understand his city? Should we follow Kafka's biographical and his city's topographical facts? Prague was where Franz Kafka was born, went to school, became a lawyer and worked. But in his writings it was also a timeless metaphor for the kind of life he felt his city forced him to live. Prague exerted relentless pressure, which Kafka constantly felt. For Kafka, Prague turned into a complex web of obstacles that blocked his path at every turn. Prague was where Kafka had to suffer the "inescapable anathema" of his double life, which encompassed his need to write and his job as a lawyer.

In his stories, Kafka named no places or landmarks of his native city. The greatest "obscurer" in modern literature, Kafka cared little about his readers gaining a definite image of Prague. Instead he treated us with his unique ambiguity that turned Prague into a visionary symbol transcending reality. So, where do you start if you want to understand Kafka's relationship with Prague?

End as starting point

Kafka never escaped Prague. Though he died in a tuberculosis sanatorium in Vienna on June 3, 1924, one month short of his forty-first birthday, his remains were brought back to Prague for burial. His grave is where your journey into Kafka should start: take the Metro Line A to the Zelivskeho Station, then walk to the entrance to the Jewish section (Novy Zidovske hrbitovy) of Strasnice Cemetery. Unlike the small and overcrowded ancient cemetery in Prague's Jewish Quarter, this one, laid out in the 1880s, is one of Prague's largest. The Kafka family plot is about 600 feet to the right of the entrance.

A family tombstone designed in Czech Cubism style marks the plot: father Hermann joined his son in 1931; the writer's mother, Julie, died in 1934. In death, as in their anguished lives, all three are together. The small tablet at the gravesite also commemorates Kafka's sisters. All three perished in the Holocaust. On the wall opposite the grave a simple plaque recalls Kafka's lifelong friend Max Brod who, in spite of Kafka's wishes, published most of his manuscripts posthumously. Without Max Brod, Kafka would most probably have remained unknown, read only by a few German-speaking intellectuals in Prague, Vienna, and Berlin.

Writing was a very personal process for Kafka. Whether he was published or how many read him was never his concern. "Writing," he once mentioned to his friend Johannes Urzidil, "is a form of prayer. Even if no redemption comes, I still want to be worthy of it every moment" (*There Goes Kafka*). Kafka's recognition as one of the greatest writers of the twentieth century began after his death and grew during the years before and after World War II. In the 1950s, the Soviet Union's dominance over the Eastern Bloc countries forced his works underground. After the fall of the Berlin Wall and the Velvet Revolution in Prague in 1989, Kafka became Prague's favorite son, a saint, martyr, god of modernism, and a prime tourist attraction.

However, hardly a single guidebook published in U.S. mentions Kafka. Finding Kafka in Prague is a personal journey of discovery.

Kafka's Prague as a small circle: Old Town

Once, looking out from his room in Old Town Square, Kafka said to his friend and Hebrew teacher Friedrich Thieberger: "Here was my secondary school, over there…the university and a little further to the left, my office." Then, as Johannes Urzidil recalled in his memoir *There Goes Kafka*, Kafka drew a small circle in the air with his finger and added, "My whole life is confined within this small circle."

In the center of the Old Town Square (Staromestske Namesti) is a massive monument to a man who has been a Czech hero for almost six hundred years: Jan Hus. A university professor and a preacher, he predated the Protestant Reformation by a century and was burned at the stake for heresy in 1415. In 1915, Kafka most surely witnessed the unveiling of the monument in commemoration of the 500-year anniversary of Hus's death. He could have been amused by an ironic (Kafkaesque?) twist of history: a monument to the greatest of Protestants peacefully coexisted with the St. Mary's Column, a symbol of the Counter-Reformation, placed near the center of the Square. In 1918, an anti-Catholic (anti-Habsburgs) mob pulled the column down, and today it stands humbly behind the Tyn Church on the same square.

This was Kafka's world. The architectural landmarks of the Old Town Square included the contents of Kafka's "confined...small circle:" the gothic Tyn Church where Hus preached; Old Town Hall with its Apostle Clock, which has a chilling stereotypical medieval Jewish money lender among its grotesque figurines; and the Kinsky Palace where Kafka went to secondary school and where his father later owned a shop. Kafka's mother, Julie, lived in number 548/1 on the Square before marrying Hermann Kafka, the writer's father. There used to be a cafe (demolished after World War II) next to the Tyn Church that was managed by Kafka's great-uncle Leopold. At the entrance to Celetna Street, one of Prague's ancient streets, was the office of attorney Dr. Richard Lowy, where the newly-graduated lawyer Franz Kafka began his legal career.

Old Town: birthplace and education

The house where Kafka was born on July 3, 1883 was located on the north-east side of the square, very close to the Baroque Church of St. Nicholas, right at the edge of the Jewish Ghetto. The family lived there for less than a year after Franz's birth, and later moved to various locations throughout the Old Town. The house burned down at the end of the 1880s and was replaced with another building that still had the original portal. In 1965, in the atmosphere of the approaching "Prague Spring" of 1968, a memorial plaque with Kafka's bust was mounted next to the portal: Communist bureaucrats were beginning to grudgingly acknowledge the writer, though only as a critic of bourgeois morality and alienation.

During Kafka's early childhood, his family lived in a 17th-century house, called the House of the Minute (Minuta). Adorned with beautiful Italian Renaissance style frescos with biblical and classical themes, Minuta is located to the left of the Old Town Hall. From this house, little Franz used to walk every day to his elementary school. Kafka later described his early school years as "horror" (*Letter to His Father*).

To increase his son's chances of gaining a good position in the hierarchy of the imperial civil service, Hermann Kafka sent Franz to the Imperial and Royal Old Town German Secondary School in the Kinsky Palace (Palac Golz-Kinskych). Kafka's experience there was far better than at the elementary school: among his classmates was

Max Brod, who became his lifelong friend. Just before the start of World War I, Hermann Kafka moved his thriving haberdashery business to the ground floor of the same building, and in *Letter to His Father*, Kafka wrote about his feelings of "torment and shame" concerning his father's harsh treatment of the store's clerks.

In February of 1948, from the balcony of the Kinsky Palace, Communist Prime Minister Klement Gottwald announced the dismissal of all bourgeois ministers and proclaimed the birth of Communist Czechoslovakia. Now, this Old Town Square building with its pleasant Rococo facade houses a collection of paintings from the National Gallery; a Czech bookstore is located where Hermann Kafka's business used to be.

At the corner of Celetna Street and Old Town Square is the Unicorn House (U Jednorozce) where the salon of Berta Fanta used to be. An assimilated Austro-Hungarian Jewish intellectual, a poetess and a writer, Berta Fanta turned her house into one of the cultural centers of Kafka's Prague. During these gatherings, attended by prominent Jewish intellectuals like Albert Einstein, guests discussed and debated Nietzsche and Kant along with the spiritualism and teachings of Indian sages. While Kafka was mostly a silent listener, he came regularly with his friends Max Brod or Hugo Bergmann.

Not far from Old Town Square, on Zelezna Street is the Carolinium, one of the oldest buildings on the campus of Charles University, where Kafka studied law. One of the oldest universities in Europe, it was founded in 1348 by a Hapsburg: Charles IV, King of Bohemia and Emperor of the Holy Roman Empire. In the Austro-Hungarian Empire, a university-educated Jew who did not want to be baptized but aspired to a career in the civil service could choose from only two professions: medicine or law. Having been pressured by his father into choosing law, Kafka, who received his doctor of law degree in 1906, compared his legal studies to being fed with "sawdust that had already been chewed by a thousand mouths" (*Letter to His Father*).

In addition to being the seedbed of Kafka's internal anxieties and conflicts, Old Town encompassed his very special biographical circumstances. At the time of his birth, Prague was a capital of the Kingdom of Bohemia and part of the expansive Austro-Hungarian Empire; at the time of his death, Kafka was a citizen of the new Chezhoclovak Republic. He was a Prague-born Jew, yet he spoke and wrote in German. In his letter to Milena Jesenska, his Czech translator and the only non-Jew among his lovers, Kafka wrote: "German is my native language …but Czech is far more endearing" (*Letters to Friends, Family, and Editors*).

In Kafka's other letters to Milena, he described the events he witnessed as a German-speaking Jew in the newly independent republic: the growth of nationalism, workers' demonstrations, and the destruction of archives in the Jewish Town Hall in the Jewish Ghetto. "I now walk along the streets, and bathe in anti-Semitism," he wrote in 1920. "*Prasive plemeno* (filthy race) I have heard the Jews referred to" (*Letters to Friends, Family, and Editors*).

Jewish Quarter (Josephof) and Jewish identity

Kafka's identification with his Jewish heritage was very complex and Jews are conspicuously absent from his writing. In his late twenties, Kafka's interest toward his roots was sparked when he happened to see the performances of an impoverished Yiddish theatrical troop from Poland. Kafka befriended the group's lead actor, Yitzchak Lowy. Trying to promote what the intellectual Prague Jews considered lowbrow culture, Kafka organized a lecture presented by Lowy in the Jewish Town Hall in 1912. Thirty years later, Lowy died in Auschwitz.

The Jewish Town Hall can be visited today as part of the Jewish Museum complex in Prague (Zidovske Muzeum Praha). This large area, home to several synagogues and the ancient Jewish cemetery, is called Josephof and is the largest and best preserved Jewish quarter in Europe. Josephof owes its survival to the crazy whim of Hitler who planned to establish a museum of Jews as a degenerate and extinct race, a truly Kafkaesque twist of history.

Shortly after the First World War, Kafka began learning Hebrew from his friend Friedrich Thieberger, a scholar and son of a rabbi. Kafka's other close friend, Johannes Urzidil, however, did not attribute these Hebrew lessons to Zionistic aspirations but rather to Kafka's "insatiable urge for the nearness of God" (*There Goes Kafka*). It was not until Kafka's first attacks of tuberculosis, around 1917, that he began talking and writing about the Zionist cause and immigration to Palestine.

Kafka's family was more secular than traditionally observant, and Kafka blamed his father for turning Judaism into a "mere trifle, a joke....You went to the temple four days a year, where you were...closer to the indifferent than to those who took it seriously" (*Letter to His Father*).

Kafka and his father actually attended two temples in the Jewish Quarter: the Old-New Synagogue and the Pinchus Synagogue, both now within the Jewish Museum complex. The Old-New Synagogue was built in the 13th century and is the oldest still-functioning Jewish house of worship in Europe. This synagogue is shrouded in the peculiar Prague-style mystery, so well embodied in Kafka's writing. The Old-New Synagogue is linked to one of the most famous Czech Jews: 17th-century Rabbi Yehudah Loew. This Rabbi is said to be the creator of the Golem, a clay-made artificial being with supernatural powers who protected the city's Jews against acts of violence. The works of many writers, including Mary Shelly, Karel Capek, and Terry Pratchett, have been influenced by the creature. Legend says that the Golem's remains are hidden in the Old-New Synagogue. The Rabbi is buried in the Old Jewish Cemetery.

In Gustav Janovich's Conversations with Kafka, Kafka mentioned one day passing by the Old-New Synagogue: "[It] already lies below ground level. But men will go further. They will try to grind the synagogue to dust by destroying the Jews themselves."

The Pinchus Synagogue, second oldest in the Jewish Quarter, dates back to the 16th century. After World War II, it was dedicated to the 80,000 Czech Jews who perished in the Holocaust. Their names and those of the concentration camps where they were killed are written on the walls inside the sanctuary.

New Town: "the anathema of double life"

Near the Powder Tower, built as part of the medieval city walls, and where Kafka used to meet his friend Max Brod after work, the Old Town ends and the New Town begins. It was laid out by Charles IV in 1348 as a market center. In Kafka's time, New Town, with its numerous theaters, discussion societies, and coffeehouses, was in the center of the unique Czech-German-Austrian-Jewish intellectual synthesis that constituted Kafka's cultural universe.

Despite Kafka's tortured perception of his "double life" as a lawyer by day and a writer by night, he was highly respected during his fourteen years (1908-1922) as an analyst of industrial accidents for a major insurance company. The company, Workers' Accident Insurance Institute for the Kingdom of Bohemia in Prague, was located at the heart of the New Town, near Wenceslas Square (Vaclavske Namesti) at No. 7 Na Porici Street. Even though he was paid well and his work day ended in the early afternoon, Kafka was unhappy. "If one evening my writing has gone well, the next day in the office I burn with impatience and can't get anything done," he wrote to his fiancée Felice Bauer, to whom he was twice engaged. "This to-and-fro is getting worse and worse...unhappiness that refuses to leave me...True hell is here in the office" (*Letters to Friends, Family, and Editors*).

Within Kafka, an artist and a bureaucrat were forced to co-exist, and this was his constant tragedy. For him, the bureaucrat he had become was not only an obstacle, he was an enemy: the keeper of files who sat all day long at a tidy desk performing mundane tasks devoid of perception or feeling. Despite that, Kafka did enjoy and participated in some of New Town's numerous cultural events, most of which occurred around Wenceslas Square.

Wenceslas Square, named after the Czechs' favorite king and saint, and with his statue in the center, has always been at the core of not only New Town life but also of major events in Czech history. In 1939, Nazi tanks rolled into the Square to signify the conquest of the 21-year-old Czechoslovak Republic. In 1968, "Prague Spring" was crushed there by Soviet tanks. A small memorial commemorates the 1969 death of Jan Palach, who burned himself to death on the square to protest Communist oppression. In 1989, the independence of the new democratic country was celebrated there.

At the top of the square, is the beautiful Art Nouveau Grand Hotel Europa, known to Kafka as the Hotel Erzherzog Stefan. There, in 1912, in one of his first public readings, Kafka read from his story *The Judgment*. In that story, a young character's conflict with his father ends when the old man sentences his own son to death by drowning. "Dear parents, I have always loved you," cries out the young man in *The Judgment* as he jumps from the bridge into the river. Across from the Hotel Europa is the Lucerna, where Kafka and his friends enjoyed cabaret style performances and movies.

Behind the St. Wenceslas statue is the National Museum, to the right of which is the State Opera House, known to Kafka as the New German Theater. As a passionate theater buff, Kafka saw numerous German classical plays there.

Near the Powder Tower, at No. 16 Hybernska Street, a few steps from another Prague Art Nouveau masterpiece, Hotel K&K Central, is Cafe Arco, which was a favorite of Prague intellectuals and frequented by Kafka and Max Brod.

The Cathedral Quarter and the city: Prague in Kafka

Prague had always been the intellectual universe that nurtured, tortured, and sustained Kafka's writing. The Cathedral Quarter, a domineering, intimidating area situated across the river from the Old Town, is the best place and space for a Kafka pilgrim to come closest to understanding the city's impact on his writing.

During the First World War, Kafka used a tiny house his sister Ottla, his soul mate, rented for him in the Golden Lane (home of the medieval alchemists on Prague Castle or Hradcany grounds) as a retreat. The little blue house at No. 22 Zlata ulicka is now a Kafka bookstore. This ancient corner of Prague still feels full of mystery and mysticism. Standing there, in spite of the crowds passing by, you might start thinking about Kafka's stories and sinking deeper and deeper into his universe.

In 1915, Kafka published *Metamorphosis*, one of his most famous stories. There, a young man named Greg wakes up one morning to find he has turned into a giant insect. At the same time, Kafka was also working on *The Trial* (published posthumously), in which the main character, Joseph K., also wakes up one morning, just like Greg in the *Metamorphosis*, to a bizarre situation. A couple of civil servants come to K.'s room and accuse him of an unnamed crime (that he didn't commit) and put him under arrest, but strangely leave him free to go to work and lead his usual life. However, since Joseph K. does not know what he is accused of, he seeks the reason for these charges by passing through the unnamed city (Prague in Kafka?). Inside this city, Joseph K. goes through all stages of the surreal bureaucratic process with all its ridiculous misinformation. It is the absurd logic of the world of judicial courts—so familiar to Kafka as a lawyer—that finally leads to Joseph K.'s execution in the middle of the night in the old stone quarry. Many think that the stone quarry described in the novel was located in the Cathedral Quarter.

Reading *The Trial* back in Russia, where it was more accurately called "Process," we saw it as an indictment and prophecy of the Fascist/Communist Totalitarian State. And we fully understood that while Joseph K. never found out what he was guilty of, he came to believe in his own guilt. "Guilt is never to be doubted," pronounced Kafka in *The Penal Colony* (published in 1919). In that nightmarish story, readers encounter an ominous torture machine used for execution. In a matter of twelve hours, the machine carves into the flesh of a condemned man the text of the law he had broken. These stories illuminate a Kafkaesque universe, full of fear, pain, and always guilt: the world of violent metamorphosis and unnamed terror.

As always in Kafka, no specific place is named, but it is often assumed that the castle in The Castle is Prague Castle or that one chapter from *The Trial* takes place in the St. Vitus Cathedral located within the courtyard of the Castle grounds. There is no certainty in that and probably that does not matter: Prague landmarks illuminate the inner truth of Kafka's stories. In Gustav Janovich's *Conversations with Kafka*, Kafka said: "All art is a document, a statement of evidence." Without a doubt, the lawyer by day carried this "statement" into every letter or story the writer by night produced.

Uncovering Kafka's mysteries in the museum

For a diligent Kafka pilgrim, Prague will slowly uncover its secrets. And one of the best places to experience this revelation is the Kafka Museum (which I never saw mentioned in any guidebook). To get there, go from the Castle Quarter through the Small Quarter (Mala Strana) toward the Charles Bridge until you arrive at No. 2b Cihelna, where this unique museum (one of the best conceptual museums I have ever visited) is located.

Do not start your pilgrimage here, however. Look for Kafka in Prague first, get a feel for his city before immersing yourself in what the museum calls "The City of K." This exhibit first opened in Barcelona in 1999, then it was transferred to the Jewish Museum in New York in 2002, and in 2005 it moved to its true home, Prague. As Mr. Tomas Kasicka, museum curator, explained to me, a private company, COPA, stepped forward as the major sponsor of the exhibition's move to Prague.

This is not a typical literary exhibition, where chronologically organized artifacts, photographs, and documents in glass cases present visitors with "the facts." Instead, you encounter a metaphoric reflection of Kafka's work and life. The documents, the photographs, the quotes, the multimedia, all are there, but the words, images, light, and sound are used to immerse you in Kafka's imagination and in the metaphorical language of his writing.

The exhibit consists of two parts: Existential Space and Imaginary Topography. The former presents Kafka's life and the influence the environment he lived in had on him, the latter illustrates the transformation of real Prague into Kafka's Prague. Mr. Kasicka has sent me an impressive list of organizations and collections that provided their artifacts and materials for the "City of K": the National Film Archive, the Museum of Czech Literature, the Jewish Museum in Prague, the Library of Congress in Washington D.C., and the YIVI Institute for Jewish Research in New York.

In front of the Kafka Museum is a life-size sculpture by David Cerny, a well-known and controversial Czech artist: two urinating male figures standing on the edge of a basin resembling the outline of the Czech Republic. These two guys pee with a purpose, however: they do quotes by request. (A nearby sign explains how to use a phone to make "requests" to spell out just about anything.)

Mentally wired for some Kafkaesque connection, I thought this sculpture was a post-modern absurdist allusion to Kafka (a flesh tattooing machine in *The Penal Colony*?). Mr. Tomas Kasicka told me to relax my "Kafkaesque" grip. He explained that the "Peeing Men" sculpture was installed in the square well before the museum was established!

On that lovely, sunny, truly April day Kafka's Prague was laughing at me.

Selected Sources

Kafka, Franz. Letters to Family, Friends, and Editors. Translated by Richard and Clara Winston. New York: Schocken Books, 1977.

Kafka, Franz. Letter to His Father. Bilingual edition, New York: Schocken Books, 1966.

Janovich, Gustav. Conversations with Kafka. New York: New Directions Books, 1971.

Urzidil, Jonannes. There Goes Kafka. Translated by Harold Basilius. Detroit: Wayne State University Press, 1968.

The Kafka family plot in the Jewish section of the Strasnice
Cemetery. Courtesy of the Kafka Museum, Prague.

The place where Kafka was born on July 3, 1883 in Prague is
commemorated by a memorial plaque.

The House of the Minute in Prague where Kafka's family lived during his early childhood.

Jan Hus monument in the center of the Old Town Square in Prague also marks the center of Kafka's "small circle" of life.

View on the Old Town Square and the Tyn Church—Kafka's world in Prague.

The Old Jewish cemetery in Prague: Rabbi Yehudah Loew's grave from the 17th century. He is said to be the creator of Golem.

The 13th-century Old-New Synagogue in Prague where Kafka and his father attended services.

The Powder Tower in Prague is where the Old Town ends and the New Town begins. Here, Kafka used to meet his friend Max Brod.

Wenceslas Square, named after the Czechs' favorite king and saint, has always been at the center of major events in Czech history.

Beautiful Czech Art Nouveau style Hotel Europa in Prague. There, in 1912 Kafka read from his story *The Judgment*.

St. Vitus Cathedral in the Cathedral Quarter, Prague: it is often assumed that one chapter from *The Trial* takes place here.

The Golden Lane, home of the medieval alchemists on Prague Castle grounds. Kafka used the blue house at No. 22 as a retreat.

Kafka Museum in Prague, the best conceptual museum I have ever encountered.

The Pissing Men sculpture by David Cerny amuses the public in front of the Kafka Museum.

The ancient Jewish saint's grave in Cochin is venerated by local
Jews, Muslims, and Christians alike.

CHAPTER 3: INDIA

Jewish History Pilgrims in Search of a Happy Jewish Story

The grand epic story of the Jews of Europe often manifests itself in an endless chain of persecutions, humiliations, and mass murders: from century to century, from country to country. Perhaps in search of a happy Jewish story, we needed to change continents. Our path of Jewish History Pilgrims led us to India. This is how it happened.

"Growing" into India

I dreamt of India for years. As my husband Alex and I planned our trip, we both began to see India as the place in space and time where one comes for self-discovery and personal growth. The truth, which travel agents do not tell you, is that you have to know deep down why you are coming to India. If you do, you are bound to discover the most refined beauty and the deepest spirituality. You will start seeing India as not merely a country but a subcontinent, or rather, a universe. Travelling through that universe, you gradually learn—like peeling the onion, layer after layer—some very important truths about people, history, and myths. If you don't, you will be overwhelmed by the heat and smells, crowds and beggars, street dogs and cows, noise and dirt.

Since both Alex and I are lifelong students of art history, we started our trip with a specific agenda. Curious about the inlaid marble of Agra and love sculptures of Khajuraho, we thought we were going to India to study the country's unique temples and palaces. But something unexpected and wonderful happened. It was the tiny Jewish community of India that turned out to be the most amazing discovery, which transformed our trip into a spiritual journey instead. When we returned home, many of our friends were surprised to hear about Jews in India. "How on earth did they ever get there?" But they did. And they have been living in their Indian homeland in freedom and prosperity for well over 2,500 years.

Where did the Indian Jews come from?

The story about the Indian Jewish community is not widely known, and here it is. This community consists of three major distinctive groups: the Cochin Jews, the Bene Israel, and the Baghdadi. Each group has its own story to tell.

The Cochin Jews are considered the oldest, continuously living Jewish community in the world. They began arriving in waves from Judea 2,500 years ago, landing on the Malabar Coast of India and settling as traders near the town of Cochin in what is now the southernmost Indian state of Kerala. The first wave probably arrived in 562 BC following the destruction of the First Temple. The second wave likely came in 70 AD after the destruction of the Second Temple. The late 15th century saw the arrival of the third wave, Sephardic Jews expelled from Spain. Refugees escaping prosecution by the colonial Portuguese Inquisition in Goa, India, followed them.

The Cochin Jews have always enjoyed special protection extended by local rulers. As early as 392 AD (though some scholars maintain that this event happened much later, in the 11th century), the Hindu Raja (king) issued his permission for Jews to live there freely. He documented his decree on ancient copper plates, which are now kept in the Holy Ark of the Cochin Synagogue.

The Cochin Jews speak Judeo-Malayalam, a hybrid of Hebrew and the language of the state of Kerala. Only a few families are currently living in Cochin because most members of the once large community moved to Israel.

The Bene Israel Jews arrived 2,100 years ago from the Kingdom of Judea and settled in what is now the state of Maharashtra. The original group—either traders or refugees from the Romans—was shipwrecked and the survivors, seven men and seven women, were thrown on the Konkan coast, not far from today's Mumbai (Bombay). With no possessions and unable to speak the language, they joined the cast of oil-pressers. Ironically, they were nicknamed the "Saturday oil pressers" because they abstained from working on

Shabbat. They intermarried with mostly dark skinned locals and later were called the "black Jews" by the "white Jews" of Cochin.

The Bene Israel Jews speak Hindi and Marathi, the languages of the Maharashtra state. Once thriving and populous, the Bene Israel group now accounts for about 3,500 to 4,000 people. Most of them live in Mumbai, and only a few families live in Calcutta and Delhi. The majority of the Bene Israel, which is ten times their population in India today, moved to Israel.

The Baghdadi Jews arrived in India about 280 years ago. The name is somewhat misleading. Not all were exclusively of Iraqi origin; many came from Iran, Afghanistan, Syria, Yemen, and other Arab countries. They settled in Rangoon, Calcutta, and Bombay, and because they were rich and educated, they quickly became the wealthiest community. Also called Mizrachi (Eastern) Jews, they turned their new home cities into cosmopolitan, thriving entrepreneurial centers. Some became prominent politicians like the Governor of Goa, Jacob PVSM; others turned to philanthropy and built libraries and hospitals. The Baghdadi Jews speak Hindi, Marathi, and Bengali, the languages of the Maharashtra and Bengal states.

Whether they speak Hindi, Judeo-Malayalam, or Marathi, none of these languages has a word for anti-Semitism! Nevertheless, after 1948, when India gained independence from Great Britain and after the birth of the State of Israel, most of India's Jews, the Baghdadi, Bene Israel, and the Cochin, left their Indian homeland. They moved out because after the Partition of 1948, Indian Jews found themselves in a different country, one that was burning with violence. As the tiniest of small minorities, they could easily envision being crushed between the conflicting forces of Hindu nationalism and Muslim separatism. So, they left behind a more than 2,000-year history of freedom and prosperity and began their mass exodus to the new state of Israel where they now constitute about one percent of the total population. Some chose to immigrate to the U.K. or the U.S.

Ok, our friends would say, then who is left? With so few Jews in a Hindu-Muslim country of 1.2-billion people, where would you find any Jewish-related sites today? Where would you meet the Jews themselves? Instead of a simple answer, let me take you on a journey of discovery.

Delhi/Agra

Synagogue near the tomb of a Muslim emperor

In Delhi, most tourists are encouraged to see the Emperor Humayun's Tomb, which is a World Heritage Site, and is considered to be an architectural precursor to the Taj Mahal. Nearby is a tiny, one-room building that houses the best kept secret in India's capital, the Judah Hyam Synagogue. Here is where we arranged to meet with Mr. Malekar.

Ezekiel Isaac Malekar is a prominent Delhi attorney. He is also a Jewish community leader, Rabbi, Cantor, writer, and Hebrew scholar. If you were to see him on the Upper West Side of Manhattan, you would perceive him to be a Columbia University professor. A Bene Israel Jew, his native language is Hindi, and in his perfect British English, he told us about the tiny, but close knit Jewish community of Delhi. One of the oldest Jewish communities in the world (Jews have been living in Delhi for over 2,000 years), it now numbers a little over 40 people or 10 families. The synagogue also serves the needs of expatriates working in Delhi, Israeli diplomats, and Jewish tourists. When we discussed the complexity of the Jewish identity in the Hindu-Muslim culture, the subject of Mr. Malekar's many studies, he said: "As a Jew, I have Israel in my heart, but as an Indian, India is in my blood. This is my homeland."

After leaving the synagogue, we continued our exploration of Delhi's Jewish history in, of all places, a mosque.

Jewish atheist's shrine in a mosque

Jami Masjid of Delhi is the largest mosque in Asia, build by Shah Jahan who also built Taj Mahal. It is an irony of history that both the Shah and the mosque have a curious Jewish connection. Visitors and worshipers alike enter the mosque through the grand royal entrance. At the right-hand side portal is a Muslim saint's tomb. It is dedicated to a ...Jew. His name was Sarmad, and he was from a Persian-speaking, Armenian Jewish merchant family. Sometime in the 1630s, Sarmad arrived in the courts of Shah Jahan in Delhi and Agra and became close to both the Shah and his oldest son, the heir presumptive.

Sarmad had an interesting career trajectory. He was a Jew who became a Muslim, then a Hindu and, finally, an atheist. He discovered a homosexual love, and as a result, abandoned his wealth and turned ascetic, wandering through the imperial courts as a naked fakir. A brilliant linguist, Sarmad translated the Torah into Persian. He also ridiculed all major religions of his time but was very popular as both a poet and a philosopher. Aurangzeb, an evil son of Shah Jahan who killed his oldest brothers and imprisoned his father in order to get on the throne, never forgave Sarmad for his friendship with his father and his brother. In 1661, he had Sarmad arrested and beheaded for his heretical poetry. Then, Sarmad's final and typical Indian transformation happened: he became venerated as a great Sufi, an Islamic mystic, and was buried in a shrine in Jami Masjid where the anniversary of his death is commemorated annually in a festival.

India and the Holocaust

There was another, much more recent Jewish story that we heard while in Delhi. It was told by Ezekiel Malekar when he learned that my grandmother's family perished in Poland during the Holocaust.

In the beginning of World War II, a ship with 1,200 Polish Jewish orphans and some adult guardians was not allowed to dock in Britain. However, it was sponsored by a Baghdadi Jewish philanthropist, and ended up in Bombay. But there again, the British authorities would not grant them entry without permission from London. So, the Maharaja (great king) of Nawanagar, a small princely state near the Arabian Sea (now Gujarat), accepted them as his personal guests. His name was Jam Saheb Digvijay Singhji, and he was one man who had courage and determination to make a life-and-death difference. In Maharaja's estate, the refugees were well cared for until the war ended.

In 1989, the surviving members of the group along with their children and grandchildren, returned to Gujarat from the U.S. and Israel, and dedicated a memorial to their safe haven, India's state of Gujarat. The same group returned in the year 2000 when Gujarat was badly affected by a natural disaster, and the group worked to rebuild two villages. About ten years ago Ezekiel Malekar wanted to publish an account of that unparalleled chapter in the Holocaust history and contacted the Maharaja's family for comments. Maharaja's son responded that his deceased father would not have wanted any publicity because the Maharaja thought of the Polish refugees as his own brothers and sisters and treated them as such. The story of India as a shelter for Jews during the Holocaust is not commonly known, but what a very Indian story it is.

We soon discovered that not just Delhi, but Mumbai as well proved to be a treasure trove of surprising Jewish stories and sites. Would you ever think of India's financial and movie capital as the city of the eight synagogues?

Mumbai

Jews settled in Mumbai (Bombay) in the 18th century. First, the Baghdadi arrived in the 1730s. Then, the Bene Israel began migrating from the countryside into the city in the 1740s. Today, Mumbai has the largest Jewish community in India: 3,500 to 4,000 people, most of whom are the Bene Israel. We visited two of the city's eight synagogues: Kenesseth Eliyahoo and Magen David. Both were built by the Sassons, the wealthiest family of the Baghdadi Jews. The elegant blue structure of the Magen David Synagogue was erected by David Sasson in 1861. Hanna and Eliyahoo were waiting for us inside.

Hanna and Eliyahoo of Mumbai

Hanna Shapurkar and Eliyahoo Benjamin showed us the imposing Magen David Synagogue. Hanna is an art historian and a tour guide. She is petite, vivacious, and outspoken. We talked about our families and the food we like to cook for the holidays. "Yeeeak, beef!" she grimaced when I told her about my usual holiday brisket. Hanna said that though she is Jewish, she would never eat meat of a cow, a holy animal for the Hindus. Her family cooks mutton for Rosh Hashanah. We also talked about Jewish education in India and the importance of the JCC as a unifying center for the young Jews of Mumbai. Like Ezekiel Malekar of Delhi, Hanna is a Bene Israel Jew.

Eliyahoo Benjamin is the synagogue's caretaker. He proudly told us about the 150-year-old history of his synagogue. At one time, his congregation did not accept the Bene Israel. "They were thought to be too dark-skinned, not pure Jewish in blood," he said. But now, when so few are left, the differences are forgotten and they often pray together, especially during the holidays. Eliyahoo is a Baghdadi Jew. His and Hannah's first language is Marathi.

Muslim youths of Mumbai defending the shul

Today, the Magen David Synagogue is located in the middle of the Muslim neighborhood. Hanna and Eliyahoo told us that during one of the Hindu-Muslim clashes, the street youngsters wanted to make sure that no one harmed the synagogue. A group of Muslim boys joined their hands and formed a protective wall across the building's gates. This is the house of God, they said.

We also visited another great Mumbai synagogue called Kenesseth Eliyahoo. It is located in the famous Colaba district, not far from major city landmarks like the Taj Mahal Hotel and the Gates of India. And this is where Hannah told us about the history of Indian Jewish philanthropy.

Jewish philanthropy

Colaba, an affluent area in the center of Mumbai, is where most of the richest members of the Baghdadi Jewish community lived, including the Sassoons, whose ancestor David Sassoon fled Iran in the early 1800's. He and his eight sons created an international commercial empire and became one of the wealthiest families in India. They also created something that never existed in India before: philanthropy. The Sassoons built synagogues and kosher shops, of course, but also schools, hospitals, and leper asylums. They erected important Mumbai landmarks such as the elegant Flora Fountain and the Venetian Gothic-style David Sassoon Library. After visiting the Kenesseth Eliyahoo Synagogue, we went to the Sassoon library's imposing reading room, absorbed its colonial splendor, and reflected upon the impact the Jews made on so many world cultures. And now, to meet the members of the oldest, continuously living Jewish community in the world, we had to leave cosmopolitan Mumbai and fly to the south of the country, to the town of Cochin.

Cochin

One-street Jew Town and the foreigners' shul

The oldest continuously inhabited Jewish community in the world dates back 2,500 years. Today, it consists of a few families living in the Jew Town part of the port city of Cochin in the southernmost state of India called Kerala. The Jew Town is just one long, north-south street lined with shops and boutiques, some of which have signs like "N. X. Jacob Tailoring." The street is called Synagogue Lane, and this is where we go to meet Mrs. Salem.

Reema Salem

Reema lived all her life on Synagogue Lane. She looked a lot like my late mother: tiny and pale, an elegant lady in her eighties. She and I talked about Canada, where her children and grandchildren lived, and Cochin, which she said she would never leave because this was her real home, where she was surrounded by her many friends: Jews, Muslims, and Christians. The Salems, Reema's husband's family, were among the oldest families of Cochin, tracing their ancestry to the first arrivals from the Kingdom of Judea 2,500 years ago. Reema herself came from the *Paradesi* (foreigners), the Sephardim running away from the persecution in Spain and Portugal in the late 15th, early 16th centuries. Both Reema's and her husband's families are Cochin Jews. Their native language is Judeo-Malayalam.

I bought a book from Reema that Abraham Salem wrote about the 450-year-old Cochin Synagogue. I remembered seeing its model displayed in the Diaspora Museum in Tel Aviv. Then, Reema showed us where her street ended and the synagogue stood. The synagogue has the most remarkable Clock Tower with different clock faces on every one of its four walls. The clock facing the street displays Roman numerals for merchants, the one facing the synagogue has Hebrew letters, the third side facing the harbor has Malayalam numerals, and the forth dial is blank. The "foreigners," the Spanish Sephardim (Reema's ancestors) built the synagogue in 1568.

The Paradesi Synagogue is the most popular site in Cochin. Most of the tourists are Indians. The synagogue structure is unique and resembles Kerala Hindu temples, which are very different from the other Hindu temples throughout the subcontinent. The red-tiled roof covers two of the synagogue's whitewashed buildings, and the entrance is a plain wooden door leading to a treeless courtyard. The caretaker, Mr. K. J. Joy told us that the courtyard is used for Simhat Torah processions just like Hindu temple courtyards are used for their celebrations. We were asked to remove our shoes, just like anyone should when entering a Hindu temple.

Inside, we saw the most colorful of interiors: blue tiles from China cover the floor (every tile is different); silver and brass chandeliers from Belgium hang from the ceiling, along with multitude of oil lamps of every possible color. The Holy Ark, a work of art made by Kerala wood carvers, houses the famous copper plates with the Raja's guarantee of all freedoms for Cochin Jews. The Ark is covered by a beautiful curtain. Mr. Joy told us that the curtain was made from a ceremonial dress, called mundu, that Cochin Jewish women make for their weddings or when their six-year-old son reads from the Haftorah.

They no longer have a Rabbi, but a few remaining congregants continue to pray together every Shabbat and on holidays. The synagogue is adjacent to the Krishna Temple. Mr. Joy told us that one might hear the chanting from the Temple during the prayers at the synagogue. This could be a manifestation, I thought, of a uniquely Indian harmony: two ancient civilizations, with their languages and religions blending together in peace.

Our final visit in Cochin was to the grave of an old sage.

Everybody in Cochin prays to a Jewish saint

Cochin's ancient Jewish cemetery did not survive. Small houses surround the only remaining grave memorial that is honored by many symbols brought by Muslims, Hindu, and Christians. The people of India are the most pious and tolerant, we are told. They come to pray, bring their grievances, and ask for favors from an ancient Jewish saint, said to have divine powers. The sign reads in Hebrew: "...the abundance of the light of his wisdom ("Torah") shines on all communities...let his soul be in the bundle of the living (ה"תנצב), his rights will protect us, Amen (א"זי"ע)..." (Translated by Hanoch

Ben-Yami, PhD, Chair, Philosophy Department, Central European University, Budapest, Hungary).

Our Jewish story-seeking path took us through Delhi, Mumbai, and Cochin. All our new friends are members of the tiniest among the smallest Indian minorities: the Jews of India. They are the least known among the Diaspora and arguably—the most interesting. "These new friends," our U.S. friends continue asking, "are they Indian or Jewish?"

Who do they think they really are?

The truth about the Jews of India is that they are both fully Jewish and, at the same time, fully Indian. How did they manage that? I found the best answer in the writing of Nathan Katz, the world's leading authority on the Jewish communities in India and a pioneer of Indo-Judaic studies.

Dr. Katz maintains that Indian Jews formed their historic identity based on myths and legends that they continue to tell about themselves. These stories relate events that may not be purely factual, but they serve to organize people's perceptions into meaningful experiences. Just like many of us who may talk about World Wars I and II as pivotal events in our family histories, the Cochin and the Bene Israel Jews talk about their arrival in India over 2,000 years ago as though these events are still fresh in their memory. And they are.

The Cochin Jews' ancestors might have been traders or refugees from the invaders who destroyed the Temple, either the First or the Second. The first Bene Israel might have run away from the Romans, or they could have been people of commerce. And they might be neither. As far as I know, nothing supports any of these stories, but at the same time, nothing contradicts them. Actual facts are not really relevant when we deal with identity; it is the two thousand-years old narrative, the stories people tell about themselves over many generations, which create that identity. "Peoples' historical self-understanding shapes their identity more than mere history," says Dr. Katz. Because the person you are now depends on whom you think you were very long ago.

What can we learn from the Jews of India?

On a personal note, the stories of the Jews of India prompted me to think of how my own Jewish identity was formed: "Aggressors, murderers, Zhidy parshivue (wretched kikes)!" It was the Six-Day War in Israel, and in Soviet Russia two little girls, my friend and I, were desperately trying to shrink, to become invisible, when crossing the courtyard of our development. Our hearts were pierced by angry stares and shrieks of those, who just yesterday, were kind neighbors. Over four decades after that event, when Alex and I came to India, we uncovered a unique chapter in Jewish history, the happiest of Jewish stories ever told. As Dr. Katz states, the tiniest of India's communities managed to live happily in freedom while preserving their religious and cultural identity without either rejecting or being overwhelmed by the larger society they lived in.

How was this possible? Can this be explained by the acceptance and tolerance of Hindu? Or was this due to the creativity of the Jews themselves who created their own myths of origin while managing to adopt local customs?

The Indo-Jewish stories might lead us to think of something highly important for many a Diaspora Jew: acculturation versus assimilation. For many Jews, like my family and myself, who immigrated to the U.S. from socialist countries, acculturation— understood as becoming part of the society while retaining one's own religious and historical identity—was never an option. The loss of that identity as the pre-requisite to acceptance or assimilation was our only way. Being Jewish in the old country was an obstacle to overcome, a stamp in your passport preventing you from achieving your full potential. In the new country, all we ever wanted was to mutate from "immigrants" to "true Americans," whatever that meant. Few were able—or willing—to find their religious identity. But is it true only for former Soviet Jewish immigrants? Numerous recent books and studies lament either the disappearance of the American Jewry or the decline of the strength of the Jewish identity. No Indian Jew would ever be able to relate to that issue.

Our trip to India gave us more cultural and spiritual treasures than we could have ever expected. It affirmed our original belief that India indeed proved to be the place for self-discovery and personal growth in a way that could not be matched by any other country.

Selected Sources

Bhatti, A., Voight, J. H. Editors. Jewish Exile in India: 1933-1945. Delhi, 1999.

Cohen, S. M. A Tale of Two Jewries: The "Inconvenient Truth" for American Jews. Steinhardt Foundation for Jewish Life, 2006

Dershowitz, A. M. The Vanishing American Jew. Little Brown and Company, 2000.

Katz, N. The Last Jews of Cochin: Jewish Identity in Hindu India. University of South Carolina Press, 1993.

Katz, N. Who are the Jews of India? University of California Press, 2000.

Keay, J. A History of India: Revised and Updated. Grove Press, 2011.

The India of our dreams: eternal beauty of the Taj Mahal in Agra.

The India of our dreams: mysterious love sculptures of Khajuraho.

Palace of the Winds in Jaipur, Rajasthan. Exotic desert palaces of Rajasthan were that quintessential India we sought to find.

Emperor Humayun's Tomb in Delhi is considered to be an architectural precursor to the Taj Mahal.

Judah Hyam Synagogue is the best kept secret of Delhi: it is located right near the tomb of the Muslim Emperor Humayun.

Judah Hyam Synagogue interior. This one room synagogue serves the Delhi Jewish community of about 40 people.

The author with Mr. Ezekiel Isaac Malekar, a prominent Delhi attorney, Jewish community leader, Rabbi, Cantor, and Hebrew scholar.

A magnificent view of the Gates of India and the celebrated Taj Mahal hotel, Mumbai.

Jami Masjid of Delhi is the largest mosque in Asia, built by Shah Jahan. Both the Shah and the mosque have a Jewish connection.

Sarmad Tomb, Jami Masjid mosque, Delhi. Courtesy of Anoop Yadav.

The Mumbai Mogen David Synagogue was erected in 1861 by David Sassoon from one of the wealthiest Baghdadi Jewish families.

The Mumbai Mogen David Synagogue. The Torah scrolls inside the Holy Arc were brought from Baghdad by the Sassoon family.

Inside the Mumbai Mogen David Synagogue. Mr. Eliyahoo Benjamin, a synagogue caretaker (left) and Hanna Shapurkar, a tour guide (right), proudly show us around the synagogue.

Kenesseth Eliyahoo Synagogue. Another house of worship built by the Sassoon family in Mumbai.

Inside Kenesseth Eliyahoo Synagogue.

Flora Fountain. This elegant Flora Fountain in the middle of Mumbai is an example of the Sassoon family's philanthropy.

David Sassoon Library. This imposing Victorian-era Mumbai landmark was built by the Sassoon family.

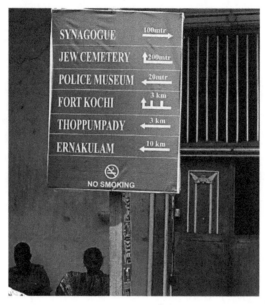

The sign on Synagogue Lane in one-street Jew Town of Cochin where the oldest Jewish community in the world still lives.

Inside an old house on Synagogue Lane in Cochin. A Passover plate adorns the wall near the door.

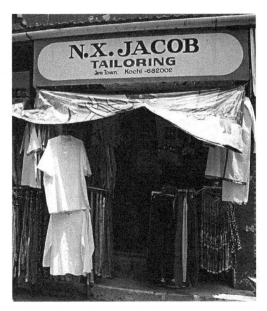

A Jewish tailor's shop on Synagogue Lane, Cochin.

The Clock Tower of the Paradesi Synagogue has four different faces. The clock facing the Synagogue has Hebrew letters.

Inside the Paradesi Synagogue of Cochin: Chinese tiles and
Belgium chandeliers adorn the interior.

Eternal light in front of the Holy Ark and a curtain made from a
woman's ceremonial sarong (*mundu*) in the Paradesi Synagogue.

The stela in front of Mr. Jin's memorial commemorating his Jewish family history in Kaifeng.

CHAPTER 4: CHINA

The Dao of Being Jewish

"Judaism is ... a precious stone which needs to be discovered, mined, and delicately carved into an intricate masterpiece." Aaron Nankin

When our friends from Chicago informed us that their youngest son was getting married and the wedding would be in Beijing, we knew instantly that we would not miss the opportunity to visit China once again. Of course, our dear friends' son's wedding was of great importance. However, I am also convinced that nothing ever happens by chance. There are no coincidences, but rather a web of connections that inevitably brings us, strangers, together and creates unmissable opportunities. That was our *Dao.*

For the Chinese, the word *Dao* or *Tao*, represents a fundamental concept of cultural philosophy that signifies the way or the path to life-long self-discovery. The October 2012 Russian-Jewish-Chinese wedding in Beijing happened shortly after our acquaintance with the Jews of India, so it was only natural that our way would then lead us to China, to seek another little-known and little-understood page in the history of the Jewish Diaspora, that of the Chinese Jews.

My husband and I came to China to share in the simha, or our friends' happiness, at the wedding, but also in search of a Jewish story. And the story we found was much more than we could have ever anticipated. It made us feel overwhelmingly blessed and nourished by the unique perception and value of Judaism we discovered in this Chinese culture, a culture much different from ours. After the wedding, our first destination was the Henan province in the central part of the country.

Kaifeng, Henan province

By Chinese standards, Kaifeng is a small town of 600,000 people in the 100 million-people province of Henan, one of the poorest in the country. There ancient capitals of a great civilization rose and fell over many centuries, nourished and ruined by the moody Yellow River. Don't look for Beijing-style skyscrapers in Kaifeng. Deep foundations for such buildings would destroy the remains of ancient cities below. Not far from Kaifeng, you can find China's oldest Buddhist temple, White Horse Temple, and one of the world's most precious collections of Buddhist cave carvings, Longmen Caves. It was in Henan, not far from Kaifeng, that the philosophy of peace— Buddhism, and the *Dao* of martial arts—Kung Fu, forged an unlikely alliance and made the Shaolin Temple the world-famous center of Kung Fu. Kaifeng served seven dynasties as a capital and became one of the world's biggest cities during the Northern Song (10th to 13th century). Kaifeng is also the capital for Jewish history pilgrims in China.

Many Jewish tours center on Shanghai as a safe haven during the Holocaust. In Shanghai, you learn about the Jews in China. To learn about the Jews of China you find no guidebook to provide you with a ready-made itinerary. No site survived to showcase that fascinating aspect of Chinese history, and modern China does not recognize its Jews as one of the country's minorities. You have to come to Kaifeng to find and meet them and hear their stories.

Mr. Jin's family tomb

Mr. Jin is a middle-aged man with a shy, kind smile. He climbed into our car on one of Kaifeng's busy streets and in rapid Chinese, shouted to our driver, "This is the way." And away we went. The smoke-laden city disappeared and a narrow bumpy road brought us into what seemed to be a different world altogether. It was not just countryside, but some silent place lost in time, dipped in a strange glow; yellow dust on the road, yellow clay on small houses, and yellow grass surrounding them. Dogs and goats were slowly crossing the street to join the children playing in the middle of it. No one moved an inch to give way to our approaching car. They too were enveloped in yellow light and golden-colored dust. "This is where,"

Mr. Jin said through the interpreter, "the Jews of Kaifeng, who settled in this city during the Song Dynasty (10th to 13th century), buried their dead for centuries." We had arrived at the oldest Jewish cemetery in China, Guang Zhong, Jin's family burial place.

We followed Mr. Jin to the small wooded area surrounded by fields and came to a black marble stela, about three-feet tall, with an engraved menorah on top. "The First Monument of Jews," announced the stela in Chinese and English. Behind it, on a pedestal of cement was a massive, five-foot tall, memorial wall, also constructed of black polished marble. "Jin Family Pedigree," read the title at the top. This marble wall was a memorial book, which presented—engraved in English on one side and in Chinese on another—the 900-year story of Mr. Jin's family within the context of Chinese history. "Chronological" (narrative) and "Genealogical" (family tree) records were written there large and flamboyant, and in stone.

This is what we learned from Mr. Jin and his marble book. Sometime in the beginning of the 12th century, Mr. Jin said, his first forebear, a Jewish trader on the Silk Road, entered China via India, and settled in what was then called Dongiing or Bianliang (Kaifeng). He was not a pioneer by any means: there already was an established small but thriving Jewish community in Kaifeng. A rich person, that first patriarch bought a family plot south of the city walls, in a place called Caizhuang.

The family's original name was lost in time. But we learned how Jin's ancestors along with other Chinese Jews got their current names. The first Emperor of the Ming Dynasty (1368-1644), who liberated China from the Mongols and hated all foreigners, forced Jews to assume Chinese surnames. And this is how Mr. Jin's family name became Jin. It was an occupational name, he explained, an equivalent of Goldsmith. Also, at that point, Jewish men started to intermarry with their Chinese neighbors and paternity became the accepted rule in determining the Jewish origin.

We continued to follow Mr. Jin's family's illustrious story and read about an "Honorable Minister of Salaries" in the 1300s; a high-level army officer, a "Vanguard Commander" in the 1400s; and a Confucian scholar in the 1600s. One ancestor financed rebuilding of the Kaifeng Synagogue when it was ruined by a flood, another paid for the repair of its ancient Hebrew scrolls. The Nationalist era

(1912-1949) and the Revolution saw the family's fortune reversed: there were opium addiction and a suicide, an inheritance was squandered and land lost or taken by the government. The Jews of China: officials and merchants, generals and scholars, shop owners and farm laborers—some rising to great success, some swept away and destroyed by the current of history—they all became alive in our imagination, reaching out to us through the letters engraved on marble and Mr. Jin's voice.

"Here are my immediate family members," said Mr. Jin, pointing out numerous unmarked little mounds around us. "My father is here and my brother is over there." While most of his family members immigrated to Israel, Mr. Jin chose to stay in Kaifeng, dedicating all his life savings and indeed most of his life to building this monument. "In our tradition," he said, "[the] older generation had to pass [the] family history to the young ones. So, my siblings and I always knew that we were Jewish." And so did the Chinese government.

Every family in China is required to have a household register, called a Hukou. This system originated in ancient China, where family registers were in existence since the 3rd century BC. In modern China, these registers became mandatory in 1958, and Jin's family always registered their "nationality" as Jewish. In 1985, said Mr. Jin, the government took Hukou books away from those who considered themselves Jews and changed their nationality, in case of the Jins, to Han Chinese.

In a country that neither accepts Judaism as one of its official religions nor includes Jews among its other 56 minority groups, and in a city where the last Rabbi died over 150 years ago and no synagogue exists, Mr. Jin's family lights candles on Shabbat and abstains from pork. Sometimes on Jewish holidays, they get together with other families of a similar background. Proud of their Jewish origins, considering themselves Jewish to the core, the Jins continue telling their story. True to the Confucian culture of their country, Jin's family kept their genealogical records for many centuries.

When the government confiscated records, a secretly made copy of it was securely hidden, and then reborn as Mr. Jin's marble monument to his ancestors and to the eternal Jewish spirit.

The story of Esther, a Kaifeng Jew

This is exactly what Guo Yan Zhao prints on her business card: "Kaifeng Jew." In large bold letters, she announces to the world both her identity and her occupation. Above this brave proclamation, is a required qualifier in small letters and almost unnoticeable: "a descendant of." Guo Yan chose Esther as her Jewish name because Chinese Jews think of her as a prophetic, matriarchal figure from the Bible. Esther's card also has a photo of her wearing Magen David-shaped earrings and dressed in a traditional Chinese gown made of blue and white (Israeli colors) silk and decorated with Jewish stars. Two ancient cultures seamlessly blended together and became Esther's personality and her life's work. For every Jewish pilgrim coming to Kaifeng, this petite vivacious young woman is an institution by herself.

Esther met us in the heart of medieval Kaifeng on a narrow street called "Teaching the Torah Lane." This was a neighborhood where Jews of Kaifeng used to live and pray for almost 800 years. Now a hospital and a nursing facility stand where the ancient synagogue, first built in 1163, used to be. But this is not the end of the Kaifeng Jewish story. Not as far as Esther is concerned. The copper plaque next to the street's name proclaims "Here live Kaifeng Jews (the Zhao residence)." Zhao is Esther's family name.

"I love both of my cultures," said Esther as she led us along the old street to her family house. "You know why? Because we are the two oldest civilizations in the world and we share a lot in common." As Esther put it for us, both Jews and Chinese have large diasporas outside of their homeland; both peoples emphasize the high importance of family ties and education (a "sacred pursuit," Esther said), and both are marked by an entrepreneurial spirit. And a talent to survive and persevere, she added. "The Chinese government never recognized us as Jews," continued Esther, "and the rabbis today never considered us Jewish either." She looked at us almost defiantly: "But we are THEY, the Chinese Jews, the Kaifeng Jews." Out of her handbag, she took out a worn photocopy of DNA test results done in the late 1980s when about 90 Kaifeng Jewish decedents were tested. "See here," she said. "We are as Jewish as you are." Learning that my husband and I were both former Soviet émigrés, she could not resist: "More so than the Soviet Jews who intermarried both ways. Not just along the male line like us."

Like her Biblical namesake, Esther is on a mission. "It is my job," she proudly stated to us, "to bring back a strong sense of Kaifeng Jewish tradition and not let it become lost in history as it did before." And Esther has a plan. Long-term, she submitted to the government her ambitious proposal to rebuild the synagogue and to create an Israeli-Chinese cultural park; short-term, she educates visitors, one person at a time.

A small house where Esther was born and raised, and where her family lived for generations, used to be a part of the ancient synagogue structure. Throughout the entire history of Jewish Kaifeng, said Esther, her family was charged with maintaining the synagogue, and when it was ruined by recurring floods, with supervising its reconstruction. Now, her house bears a proud name: The Kaifeng Jewish History Memorial Center. The centuries-old doorframe proudly displays a mezuzah and the door is adorned with a small Israeli flag. The first thing we saw when entering the house was a large banner with the Shema prayer, a central statement of Jewish theology, written in golden letters: "Hear O Israel, the Lord is our God, the Lord is one."

Esther explained that during the Ming Dynasty, around the 14th or the 15th century, the Chinese Emperor demanded that his portrait be placed in every house of worship. So, the Kaifeng Jews had no choice but to obey, and they placed the portrait in the entryway to the synagogue, but above it, they hung a Shema. In Kaifeng, the God of the Jews was above even the all-powerful Emperor of China!

The Jewish history center we entered was a one-room display of numerous family photos, documents, booklets, and articles on Chinese Jewish history in Hebrew, Chinese, and English. They were all surrounded by menorahs, Shabbat candlesticks, and Israeli flags. A large framed rendering of the Kaifeng Synagogue by an 18th-century Jesuit priest was proudly placed in the center of the back wall. Underneath it stood a wooden model of the synagogue as shown in the Tel Aviv Diaspora museum. We bought a nicely illustrated brochure authored by the "Kaifeng Jew Esther" about the history of the synagogue and the History Center she created.

Esther began her story with the Name, not her family name, but the names the Jews were called in China, their new home country.

The names were important because how your neighbors called you said a lot about how you were perceived and accepted. Having grown up in the Soviet Union, we remembered very well how our neighbors called us *Zhidy* (Kikes) and "Israeli aggressors," so we could not agree with her more.

The sinew-plucking religion

Chinese people never had prejudice against foreigners coming down the Silk Road or those settling in their midst. Whether they were Jews or Muslims from Persia or Christians from the West, the Chinese called them all "people with colored eyes." When the Jews settled in Kaifeng, they were called *Lan Ma Hui Hui*, which meant "Blue Hat Muslims" because of the blue hats they wore when going to the synagogue.

"White Hat Muslims" was the name for those who wore white hats when praying at the mosque. To add to this confusion, both Muslims and Jews gave the same Chinese name to their houses of worship: *Qing Zhen* or "Pure Truth." Though neither ate pork, the Jews also prepared their meat in accordance with Kashrut Law: removing the thigh muscles (sinews) from the hip sockets of the slaughtered animals. It was done in reference to the Biblical story of Jacob sustaining a thigh injury while wrestling with an angel. That was so peculiar to their Chinese neighbors that the Jews became *Tiaojinjao*—the religion that removes the sinew.

All these names were given just to describe people with different customs and to distinguish between them, never with animosity or violent hostility. The Chinese word for Jew, *Youtai*, was not used in China until the Jesuits introduced it in the 17th century. "But we," Esther said, "always called ourselves "the Children of Israel" and since we were comfortable and prosperous in Kaifeng, we built our synagogue here."

The Confucian-looking synagogue

It is unknown what the first Kaifeng Synagogue built in the 12th century looked like. What we know is based on much later descriptions and drawings made by the Jesuits in the 17th century. For anyone who has visited the Forbidden City in Beijing and at least a temple or two elsewhere in China, the synagogue rendering reminds one of the country's typical residential or religious compounds. The synagogue was built according to the Confucian principles of architecture, explained Esther, and that legitimized both Jews and their faith for the country that had never known organized religion.

Just like many buildings in China, stone lions flanked the entrance to the synagogue complex consisting of enclosed courtyards and halls. The pathway to the Front Hall was also guarded by two large marble lions on pedestals. A giant iron incense tripod, like in Taoist or Buddhist temples, stood between the lions. The entire compound was described as being four hundred feet in depth. Unlike Chinese temples that face south, the synagogue gate looked eastward while the worshippers faced westward. The Great Synagogue of Kaifeng offered a full-service lifestyle: kitchen, ritual bath or mikva, study halls, meeting rooms, and lecture halls. There was the Hall of the Founder of the Religion (Abraham), Hall of the Patriarchs, and Ancestral Hall. The Main Hall was forty by sixty feet in size and like any other Chinese main hall it was raised on a platform and surrounded by a balustrade. In the middle stood a large table for an incense burner and candlesticks. A Chair of Moses was placed behind the table. The Torah raised up high was read from that place. The name for Torah in Chinese, Esther said, is *Daojing*. The word *Dao* means "the Way" and the *jing* means "the scriptures." Put together "Daojing" means "The Scriptures of the Way."

The stories told by stones

Kaifeng Jews were not the first ones to arrive in China. Historians believe that Jews already lived there during the Han Dynasty (206 - 220 AD). Jews and their synagogues are mentioned by name in a poem written during the Tang Dynasty (618-906). In the Luoyang Museum (also in the Henan province), we noticed half-a-dozen figurines made of famous Tang period tricolor ceramic. They were peddlers, bakers, and merchants with clear Semitic features. They could be Arab traders of course, who arrived via the Silk Road. But they could be Jews, also. To us, they seem quite Jewish in appearance. "Yes," said Esther, "there were other Jewish settlements in ancient China." But, "we," she stated with pride, "were the largest community in China and the one that lasted the longest and the only one which left substantial records of its own."

These records are the three large stone stelae erected to commemorate the rebuilding of the synagogue in 1489, 1512, and 1679. One more stela dated 1663 was lost, but the remaining ones are kept in a small, controlled environment, in the Kaifeng Municipal Museum where photography is prohibited. The stelae could be visited by appointment only with a private guide. Esther took us there; after a long steep climb up the stairs, we faced three large limestone stelae. Centuries old and badly damaged by rain, wind, and floods, they were there to tell their stories through protective glass. These stories are of Jews first entering China and of the Imperial welcome, their long history in Kaifeng, and interpretations of Jewish beliefs and practices. The stories were written in Chinese, said Esther, and when she read us excerpts from a handout, it became clear that the authors tried really hard to stress the similarities of their faith and practices to those of the Chinese Confucians. The founder of the Jewish religion, Abraham, is called a descendent of Pangu, a mythological Chinese character who created the universe. It is said that Abraham established the Jewish religion in the "146th year of [the] Zhou dynasty" (10th century BC) and then this religion was given to Moses, a "Patriarch of the True Religion, in the 613th year of Zhou" (5th century BC). "[The] Jewish way of worshiping God, continues the text of the 1489 stela, "fully manifested the mysteries of the Ancestral Dao...Dao has no shape or form but is above all else." The same stela recounts that the Jews arrived in China during the Song Dynasty (10th-13th centuries) from India (or the Middle East); the Emperor, who most probably was interested in cotton sold by the Jews, told them to preserve their ancestral customs and to settle in Bianliang (Kaifeng). The names of the first settlers' 70 clans are listed in Chinese, including Rabbi LeiWei (probably a Levite). The remaining two stelae mention other Jewish communities in China, emphasize the "boundless loyalty" of the Jewish soldiers to their new home country, and commemorate the rebuilding of the synagogue.

By the time the last stela was created in 1679, the Silk Road was only a memory and Kaifeng was no longer a capital. Its economic importance as an international trade center ended, and prosperity deeply declined. So did the wealth of the small Jewish community. By the mid-nineteenth century, the Kaifeng Jewish community all but disappeared. Destroyed and rebuilt many times, the Kaifeng synagogue never recovered from an 1840s flood, and by the 1850s, it was in ruins. By then, no Jew in Kaifeng could read Hebrew, and there was no Rabbi. It is known that at that time, a Torah scroll was displayed in the Kaifeng market together with a sign offering a reward to any traveler who could interpret its text for local Jews. Ancient scrolls from the synagogue were sold to Westerners and today can be seen in various museums around the world: from the British Museum and Cambridge University in the U.K., to the Royal Ontario Museum in Toronto, Hebrew Union College in New York, and the Jewish Theological Seminary in Cincinnati. The synagogue ruins were cleared and the land was sold. What is left from the Great Synagogue are the remains of the mikva inside the hospital built on its site and the story-telling stone stelae in the museum.

Why did the Kaifeng Jews disappear? And did they?

There is no single answer. Were the Chinese Jews dispersed by natural and man-made disasters, recurrent floods and wars, or rebellions and economic decline? If we look at the history of European Jewry over the centuries of persecutions and pogroms, these reasons alone could not fully explain the disappearance of the community. Was it then a historic circumstance of a community being small in numbers, isolated geographically, and overpowered by the strong Chinese culture? By comparison, if we look at India, there the Jews, the tiniest of India's communities, managed to live in prosperity and freedom for 2500 years till today. They were able to preserve their religious and cultural identity without being overwhelmed by the large Hindu-Muslim society they lived in. Was it that the cultural atmosphere in China, though hospitable and tolerant to foreigners, was not conducive to practicing Judaism? Indeed, the early signs of erosion were well documented. For example, in the Confucian-style synagogue, incense was burned to honor biblical heroes, sacrifices in the Chinese style (but of kosher food) were offered on some Jewish holidays, and boys studied Confucian texts instead of the Torah.

The existence of the Jews in China was unknown to the Western world until 1605, when a Jesuit priest, Matteo Ricci, met a Kaifeng

Jew in Beijing who arrived there to take Confucian examinations for a prestigious government post. As described by Ricci, that young man was dressed and looked Chinese but considered himself Jewish, a believer in One God. Perhaps by that time, an overwhelming number of young ambitious Jewish men, instead of dedicating their lives to Torah, preferred to study Confucius, a requirement for any promising government position. By the early 1600s, the Kaifeng Rabbi was already struggling with the lack of young men knowledgeable in Jewish law because, as Ricci recorded, the rabbi offered him a job as his successor—if the Jesuit joined the Jewish faith and stopped eating pork, of course.

"Yes," Esther told us, while we smiled at the Rabbi-and-a-Jesuit story, "We lost our ancestral language, traditions, even bloodline. But we kept our memories and pride in being Jewish. We told stories. We survived."

There are probably a few hundred people in Kaifeng now who consider themselves Jewish either through a family line or marriage. A growing number of young people discover their Jewish roots and make aliyah to Israel; Hebrew classes are highly popular in Kaifeng, and Esther told us of frequent Shabbat gatherings with a communal service, songs, and a potluck kosher (Halal) meal. At the conclusion of Shabbat, they sing Hatikva in Hebrew, often by memory. "I don't like the word assimilation," Esther said. "Are you a Jew only if you go to the synagogue and read Torah there? Do you think there is only one Dao of being Jewish?"

What we learned from the Jews of China

For Esther, Mr. Jin, and their families, the Dao to being a Jew is built on family memories, understanding of Judaism as a precious treasure, and a strong sense of identity handed down from generation to generation. And they are prepared to uphold this ancestral heirloom against any powerful force, whether cultural, political, or economic. The Jews of China helped us to see that we, Western Jews, are not just one among many minority cultures in the large societies where we live, but are an integral part of a unique, millennia-old tradition with its own historic and geographic trajectory.

Selected Sources

Goldstein, J. The Jews of China: Historical and Comparative Perspectives. Routledge, 1998.

Guang, Pan. The Jews in China. China Intercontinental Press, 2005.

Hansen, V. The Silk Road: A New History. Oxford University Press, 2015.

Keay, J. China: A History. Basic Books, 2001.

Shapiro, S. Jews in Old China: Studies by Chinese Scholars. Hippocrene Book, 2000.

The author with Mr. Jin in front of his marble memorial in Kaifeng.

The oldest Jewish cemetery in China: Mr. Jin's family's burial place in Kaifeng.

In the heart of medieval Kaifeng: this is where the Jews lived and prayed for over 800 years.

The street signs on the site of the ancient Jewish neighborhood in Kaifeng. The Great Synagogue was located behind this wall.

The Kaifeng Jewish History Memorial Center in Esther's ancestral home. This building used to be a part of the synagogue structure.

The author and Esther in front of the entrance to Esther's house in Kaifeng. The *Shema* is visible on the opposite wall.

Esther tells the Jewish story of China. On the wall is an 18th-century rendering of the Kaifeng synagogue.

The Kaifeng Municipal Museum houses three ancient stone stelae detailing the history of the Jews in China.

Luoyang, Henan province. One of the ancient great capitals of old China with one of the oldest Jewish settlements.

Tang period (618-906) ceramic figurine in the Luoyang Museum. This peddler has clear Semitic features.

At the head of the Oslo Fjord in Oslo is the striking Opera House. Walk or skateboard or sunbathe right on the roof.

CHAPTER 5: NORWAY

Exploring Scandinavian
Jewish Narrative

In 2014, with violent anti-Semitism rising in Europe, we stopped for a while our exploration of happy Jewish stories in Asia, and turned our attention to Europe. We decided on Scandinavia, a part of Europe renowned for its inclusiveness and tolerance.

Painful Journey: collecting Jewish stories of Scandinavia

A few weeks prior to the trip, I came across a December 2012 issue of *Standpoint*. As I learned from that U.K. magazine, Norway, a country that regularly tops every survey of wealth and quality of life, could soon top one more shocking ranking: the first country in Europe to become "Judenfrei," the Nazi term for the ethnic cleansing of Jews. Then a friend emailed me several intriguing 2013 documents: *Anti-Semitism in Norway?—The Attitudes of the Norwegian Population towards Jews and Other Minorities* and FRA (European Union Agency for Fundamental Rights) Survey: *Discrimination and Hate Crimes against Jews in EU Member States.* The Jews of Scandinavia seemed to be talking to me daily from my computer screen. "How to Survive as a Jew in Sweden: Shut up and Fade into the Woods," wrote Annika Hernroth-Rothstein in the *Mosaic* Journal. "Hiding Judaism in Copenhagen," corroborated Michael Moynihan in *Tablet* Magazine. At that point, I knew that our trip will become a painful journey into the past and present of Scandinavian Jewry.

Scandinavian images: where Shakespeare got it wrong

"Pray ...grant this country... from God, truly bounty and peace, blessed for mankind." Old Norse Poem

"Something is rotten in the state of Denmark," declares an officer in *Hamlet*, and this is where I thought the Bard was gravely mistaken. We visited Denmark, Sweden, and Norway in May. Everything we encountered there looked beautiful; and in spite of the cold and rain, this beauty seemed almost surreal. In the Nyhavn part of Copenhagen, brightly painted houses along the canal sparkled like jewels in the rare moments of sunlight. In Elsinore, the brooding Kronborg castle, the fictional home of Shakespeare's Hamlet, was an image of somber beauty and overwhelming power as if still threatening Sweden across the narrow gulf. In Stockholm, the Royal Palace, baroque churches, flowers in the parks, and people on the streets were all lit by an out-of-this-world grayish-bluish light as if they existed inside a magic giant crystal. In Oslo, the never ceasing rain and wind were natural architects of not only spectacular fjords around the city but also of, it seemed, its striking architecture. Oslo's dazzling Opera House resembled a giant glacier sliding into the sea: its white marble roof doubled as a public square. These are some of the iconic images of Scandinavia I brought home. I fell forever in love with this still underappreciated, under visited part of Western Europe.

Without the Scandinavians, Europe might have looked very different. The ancestors of today's Danes, Swedes, and Norwegians, the Vikings, while ruthless pirates, were also great seamen, shipbuilders, and explorers. Between 800 and 1000 AD, the Danes founded Dublin in Ireland and ruled the southern part of England. Northmen from Denmark also settled in the region of Normandy in Northern France. The Swedes went into Russia and, according to some historians, founded Nizhniy Novgorod and Kiev there. One Norwegian Viking, Eric the Red, was among the first settlers in Iceland, and his son, Leif Eriksson, is often credited with discovering North America around the year 1000 AD. In Copenhagen, we saw a car proudly displaying a bumper sticker that read: "Columbus followed [a] Viking map."

Speaking of cars, you won't find many of them in Scandinavian capitals: a sky high tax on cars (180% in Denmark) makes bicycles, buses, and ferries much more attractive. Today, the descendants of the Vikings are highly conscious of their environment: over half of their garbage is recycled and more than 20 percent of their energy needs are provided by windmills. "Copenhagen to be the World's First Carbon-Neutral capital," declared *Newsweek* in August 2014. Indeed, this part of Europe is arguably one of the most sophisticated on the continent, and Scandinavians are among the most educated and prosperous Europeans, with the least income disparity. Scandinavian countries are also the most highly taxed and socialistic, but their people, the happiest we ever met, think it works, and they consider their home countries the best places in the world. Indeed, the *2014 Legatum Prosperity Index* (the only global measure of prosperity based on both income and well-being) shows Norway in 1st place with Sweden and Denmark in 4th and 6th respectively. (The U.S. was rated 10th). Norway has kept its top place since 2009. However, as we discovered during our visit, this highly sophisticated, perfectly organized, everything-for-the-people civilization has its dark sides. Perhaps Shakespeare did know what he was talking about.

Norway – past

"This people (the Jews) always have been rebellious and deceitful... they have acquired some remarkable fortune that led them to intrigues... It is of vital importance to the security of the state that an absolute exception be made about them." One of the framers of the 1814 Norwegian Constitution.

The history of government decreed anti-Semitism in Norway goes back over a millennium. In the year 1000 AD, the Norwegian King Olav forbade everyone who was not Christian to live in Norway. But the first time Jews were specifically singled out happened in 1436, when a prohibition was issued and then repeatedly reinforced, to abolish a day of rest on Saturday, lest Christians replicate the "way of Jews." While Norway was part of the Kingdom of Denmark (1536-1814), the Danes issued numerous religious restrictions to uphold Protestantism in general and to persecute the Jews in particular. Every foreigner in the kingdom had to affirm their commitment to the Lutheran faith on pain of deportation or even death. Christian IV of Denmark and Norway (1577-1648) was a Renaissance ruler and a pragmatist. He understood the value Jewish merchants could bring and allowed some wealthy and well-connected Sephardim Jews to enter his realm. Christian V rescinded these privileges in 1687, banning Jews from Norway entirely. If found in the kingdom, Jews were jailed or expelled. This ban persisted until 1851.

In 1814, when Norway passed from Denmark to Sweden, the country had a short-lived hope of gaining independence and adopted their first Constitution. The document was written in a liberal and progressive spirit; however its second paragraph stated that the Jews were to "continue" to be excluded from the country. Henrik Wergeland, a national poet, lobbied to change this paragraph. In 1851 the ban was indeed lifted, six years after Wergeland's death. To commemorate the poet's victory over bigotry, the Jews of Oslo gather at his grave every year and have a thanks-giving service. Following the repeal, only 25 Jews immigrated to Norway before 1870. By the beginning of the 20th century though, pogroms in Russia brought about 1,000 Jews to the country.

Norway during World War II

When the Nazis invaded Norway in 1940, some 2,100 Jews lived in the country, almost all of them as fully assimilated Norwegian citizens. After the Norwegian collaborationist government took over running the country, Nazi anti-Jewish legislation was promptly implemented. To identify Jewish Norwegians, the government relied on information from the police and telegraph services, while the synagogues and Jewish burial societies were ordered to produce full rosters of their members and even non-members they knew about. The resulting lists were cross-checked against information eagerly provided by private citizens and by the Norwegian Central Bureau of Statistics. In the end, due to the enthusiastic support of the population, Norway had a more complete list of its Jewish residents than most other countries under Nazi occupation. In 1942, government organized deportation sent 772 Jews to Auschwitz, 740 of whom were murdered. To their credit, the Norwegian resistance movement succeeded in smuggling about 900 Jews to safety across the Swedish border.

Norway – present

"I would like to take the opportunity to remember all the billions of fleas and lice that lost their lives in German gas chambers, without having done anything wrong other than settling on Jewish as..s." Popular Norwegian comedian Otto Jespersen, on national television, Nov. 2008. He claimed this remark was not anti-Semitic but "just funny."

Today, around 1,400 Jews call Norway their home. About 900 of them belong to the Oslo and Trondheim Jewish communities. Oslo's Jewish community is the larger of the two. In a country with a population of five million, the Jews are the tiniest of minorities, which never prevented them from being "noticed." I compiled a "collection" of anti-Semitic acts in Norway. Here are just few examples. In January 2004, the Norwegian newspaper *Dagsavisen* printed an editorial cartoon that depicted an Orthodox Jew rewriting the Ten Commandments to include "thou shall murder." In September 2006, the synagogue in Oslo was subjected to an attack with an automatic weapon. When the shooter was convicted, he received a few years in prison for "serious vandalism." The Oslo city court judge could not find sufficient evidence that the shots fired at the synagogue amounted to a terrorist act. In January 2013, the newspaper *Dagsavisen* interviewed leaders of the Muslim community and cited their claim that the existing hostility between Muslims and Christians is caused by Jewish influence. The newspaper also quoted these leaders' beliefs that the reason the Nazis killed Jews was that they (Jews) make other people fear them.

We arrived in Oslo the same day as the President of Israel Shimon Perez began his official state visit to Norway at the invitation of the King and the Parliament. The City Hall and the main street, Karl Johan Avenue, were adorned with Israeli flags. We later learned about the protest—an anti-Israeli demonstration of 300 people—but did not see it. Just to see the Israeli flags all over this northern European capital was very uplifting. So what does it mean today to be a Jewish Norwegian?

To find the answer, or rather answers, to this question, we went to the Jewish Museum and the Holocaust Research Center, both in Oslo.

The Jewish Museum of Oslo is located in the old synagogue building on Calmeyer Street in the center of the city, in a neighborhood marked by the immigration of the last 30 years: you see an Iraqi barbershop, Kurdish bakery, and a mosque. This area was traditionally an immigrant enclave. Fleeing pogroms in Eastern Europe, about 100 Jews were the first settlers. In the building next to the museum, Salomon Selikowitz from Lithuania opened his haberdashery business in the 1890s. Most Jews who lived on this street during the 1940s ended up in Auschwitz. Today, only the "Stolpersteine" or memorial brass cobblestones with the victims' names, dates of birth, and dates of deportation attest to the destruction of the Oslo Jewry. Few people hurrying down the street look down at these brass plates. The voices of the dead are barely heard. The Salomon Selikowitz building houses a Middle Eastern restaurant.

Conversation with Lior Habash

The Museum is not easy to find; it is hidden behind locked gates. We rang the bell and were met by Lior Habash, an architecture student, who works at the Museum. The Museum houses an excellent exhibit "Remember us unto life—Jews in Norway 1940-45" dedicated to Norwegian Jews deported on the vessel Donau and then sent to Auschwitz. All signs are in Norwegian and English as you follow the stories of those who were murdered and those who were helped to survive.

Meeting with Lior was a highlight of our visit. A vivacious and delightful young man, Lior personifies modern diverse Norway. He is an Israeli by birth with a Norwegian Jewish mother and a Yemenite Israeli father. His maternal grandparents emigrated from Belorussia; some of their immediate family members perished during the Holocaust. Lior is painfully aware of the often irreconcilable duality of his own existence. "I love Oslo," he says," but I feel split in between two worlds, an Israeli and a Norwegian. It is very important for me to be a Norwegian, but I am a Jew first of all." Lior keeps kosher and cannot imagine marrying a non-Jewish girl. Asked if he feels safe to go to work every day at the Jewish Museum located in a Muslim neighborhood, Lior said "No. I do not." When unlocking the always-locked gate, he often looks over his shoulder, to check if anyone is watching him. Though Lior has a diverse group of acquaintances of Norwegians, Jews, and Muslims, he feels that Norwegians are generally very reserved, not really open to those who they see as outsiders. "They have a sort of a bubble around them," said Lior. "Not easy to penetrate it." As we part, Lior urged us to take a look at the brass cobblestones with deportees' names, a memorial, he explained, to Jewish Norwegian history. "You know," Lior said, adding a positive note as we leave, "there is a growing interest among non-Jews toward Jewish history in general and what happened during the war in particular." The museum has a number of non-Jewish members and donors, and school groups come there on a regular basis. As for Lior, he travels to Israel every year and thinks he might be moving there for good after receiving his architectural degree. A number of his Jewish friends have similar plans.

Discussing the Norwegian brand of anti-Semitism with Ann Elizabeth Mellbye

Next, we headed to the Center for Studies of Holocaust and Religious Minorities located in Bygdoy, in a beautiful wooded island just across the harbor from downtown Oslo. The Holocaust Center is located way out of the island's museum cluster, and while the Viking Ship, Folk Culture, and Kon-Tiki museums are always filled with weekend families and cruise ship crowds, we were the only visitors at the Norwegian Holocaust Center. The Center is situated in a 1917 villa; built in the National Romantic style, the building resembles a Nordic castle. In 1941, this property was acquired by the leader of the Norwegian Nazi party, Vidkun Quisling, who lived there until his arrest and eventual execution in May of 1945. The first thing we noticed when approaching the Center was the giant sculpture that resembled a punch card. Created by Arnold Dreyblatt, the artwork is called "Innocent Questions." Shifting words and phrases displayed on this giant punch card are connected to personal data, "innocent" perhaps at a first glance, but used to facilitate mass murder of Norwegian Jews.

The Center houses a Holocaust museum and is engaged in research, documentation, and education. Inside, we were met by Ann Elizabeth Mellbye, Deputy Head of Administration, who graciously offered to guide us through the Holocaust exhibit. Initially created as an educational tool for local schools, all exhibition signs are in Norwegian, and even though one can borrow an English audio guide, we were happy to follow Anne, who proved to be a wonderful guide.

The high-tech interactive exhibition documents the destruction of the Norwegian Jewish community during the Nazi occupation. What makes this exhibit different, Anne explained, is its focus on the role Norwegians played in the mass murder of their former neighbors and co-workers. Traditionally, Anne said, in history lessons, the Germans were presented as villains, while Norwegians were resistant fighters, partisans, and heroes who risked their lives trying to smuggle their Jewish compatriots to Sweden. While the stories of heroism are certainly true, and nearly 40 percent of the Jewish population was helped to escape across the border, Norwegians today have to face the fact that the collection of data on Jewish residents, arrests, and deportations were carried out by Norwegians.

The exhibition spans three floors of the building: the ground floor documents the history of anti-Semitism and racism in Europe, Norwegian Holocaust history is presented in the basement, and the "Contemporary Reflections" exhibit is located one floor above the entrance. There, video projections reflected in mirror walls encourage visitors to contemplate the meaning of the Holocaust in contemporary society. On the day we visited, a new exhibit opened dedicated specifically to the history of the Norwegian brand of anti-Semitism: the Constitutional expulsion of the Jews from the country which was not repealed until 1851.

When I shared with Ann my "collection" of contemporary anti-Semitic acts in her country, she brought us a copy of *Anti-Semitism in Norway?* the first extensive population survey focusing on the attitudes towards Jews and other minorities. The Center undertook this project in 2012, then analyzed and published the results in 2013. "Take a look, "Ann said. "While about 12.5 percent of Norwegians might be prejudiced against Jews, when compared to the rest of Europe, the prevalence of anti-Semitic views in Norway is not really high and is close to those in the U.K., Denmark, and Sweden." The report also states that anti-Semitism can be gauged by analyzing negative feelings and social distance. The survey reveals that 9.7 percent of respondents feel antipathy towards Jews, while 8 percent of the population does not want Jews as neighbors or friends.

Respondents often explained their negative attitudes towards Jews with reference to the role played by Israel in the Middle East conflict, and almost never with specific reference to Norwegian society.

Ann felt positive about the future of the Jews in Norway. The very fact of the Center's establishment (opened by the government in 2006) along with the restitutions paid by the government to either Holocaust victims or their descendants testify to the change of attitudes toward the Jews, she told us. Educational programs for schools and training for teachers are the Center's major activities in preparing a new generation of open-minded, tolerant citizens.

When we returned back home, the Jewish Museum's director, Ms. Sidsel Levin emailed me her thoughts about Perez's visit: "It was fantastic! One demonstration on Monday, about 300 people—much less protest and articles in the media than we reckoned it would be…Perez is a man of peace … it is not so easy to attack him…Our prime minister said at the press conference that Norway will increase trade with Israel (a victory over the boycott movement!) but will keep the right to criticize Israel for how they treat Palestinians."

Have we found our answers? Is the Jewish story of today's Norway all about young people leaving the country to build their lives elsewhere? Is it a narrative of a comfortable life punctuated now and then by examples of rabid Jew-hatred? Does it promote belief in extensive education as the best way to fight bigotry and to open hearts and minds?

We were not quite sure. What we were certain of, however, was that our exploration of the Scandinavian Jewish narrative could not be limited to only one country and had to go on.

Selected Sources

Derry, T. K. A History of Modern Norway. Clarendon Press, 1973.

Fure, O. B. Anti-Semitism in Norway. Background Paper. Center for Studies of Holocaust and Religious Minorities in Norway, 2003.

Liphshiz, C. "Norwegian Ex-Premier Counters Anti-Semitism Accusations, Slams Israel." Haaretz, 2009.

Yilek, J. A. History of Norway. Wasteland Press, 2015.

Oslo wants to be the best livable capital in Europe: the city's post-modern architecture of the "Fjord City" district is very impressive.

Renzo Piano's Museum of Modern Art, Oslo.

Oslo Nobel Peace Prize Center. This thought-provoking museum celebrates over 800 Nobel Peace Prize winners.

Oslo Radhuset or the City Hall (1930) is built in the Art Deco style.

Oslo Jewish Museum covered with offensive graffiti.

Oslo Jewish Museum sign.

Oslo Jewish Museum. "Remember us into Life" exhibit commemorates Jews of Norway deported to Auschwitz.

The author with Lior Habash at the Oslo Jewish Museum.

Brass memorial plates in front of the Oslo Jewish Museum commemorate those who were sent to Auschwitz.

The Center for Studies of the Holocaust and Religious Minorities in Oslo. The "Innocent Questions" sculpture is on the left.

The author with Ann E. Mellbye, Deputy Director of the Center for Studies of the Holocaust and Religious Minorities in Oslo.

The exhibit "History of Racism and Anti-Semitism in Europe" at the Center for Studies of the Holocaust and Religious Minorities in Oslo.

View on Gamla Stan, a mediaeval center of Swedish capital city,
Stockholm.

CHAPTER 6: SWEDEN

The Country of Raul Wallenberg through the Eyes of a Jewish Traveler

Our exploration of Jewish Norway raised more questions for us than answers. To see a more complete picture of a Jewish narrative within a Scandinavian context, we took an early morning flight from Oslo, Norway, to Stockholm, Sweden, the country that during World War II was a safe haven for most of the Scandinavian Jewry.

Unlike Norway or most European countries for that matter, Sweden does not have the same painful history of government complicity in the Holocaust. The image of Sweden as a noble rescuer of the Scandinavian and Hungarian Jewry and a pluralistic state that officially recognizes Yiddish as one of its five minority languages was my understanding of this country within the context of the Jewish narrative.

The reality, as we discovered during our visit, proved to be much more complicated. The 2013 European Agency for Fundamental Rights (FRA) study showed that 37 percent of Swedish Jews declared anti-Semitism increasing "greatly" over the last five years with 22 percent having personally experienced verbal insults, harassment, or even physical anti-Semitic attacks in the past 12 months. In addition, 60 percent of Swedish Jews never wear anything in public which makes them identifiable as Jews, the highest percentage of any country in the FRA study.

Are we talking about the same Sweden?

Sweden – past

"No Jews should be permitted to settle in Stockholm, or in any other part of the country, on account of the danger of the eventual influence of the Jewish religion on the pure evangelical faith." From the Ordinance signed by King Charles XI of Sweden, 1685.

The first contacts between the Swedes and the Jews, according to some sources, could be traced back to the years 700-900, when the Vikings traded with the Khazars, a Judaism-professing people, who lived between the Black and the Caspian seas. For over 700 years after the Viking age, there was no Jewish presence in Sweden, until in 1645, as documented in Royal Archives, Queen Christina employed a physician named Bendectus de Castro, a converso, whose real name was Baruch Nehemias. It seems that at that time, the Jewish question had merely a religious aspect in Sweden, and had not yet assumed the character of a race problem. If a Jewish merchant attempted to enter the country, he was ordered to leave within a fortnight or undergo a baptism. Unlike Norway, no threat of death was implied. The law changed when King Carl XII (1697-1718) realized that Jews could be a useful source of much needed funds. War-hungry Carl XII spent five years in the Bessarabian town of Bender, then under the Ottoman Turks, and accumulated large debts. When his Jewish creditors followed him to Sweden, Carl XII had the Swedish law altered so that they could settle in and conduct their religious services.

Aron Isak, an engraver from Germany, became the first Swedish Jewish citizen when King Gustav III granted him citizenship. Isak's refusal to convert— "I would not change my religion for all the gold in the world"—impressed both the Lord Mayor of Stockholm and the King. In 1782, legislation was adopted allowing Jews to settle in Sweden without converting to Christianity. A small Jewish community was established in Sweden at about that time, and the first synagogue was built in Stockholm in 1787. As Jews received their new rights and gained prosperity, the Swedes who witnessed a small and disadvantaged community growing in wealth rioted and presented numerous complaints to the government denouncing the "undue preference" towards the Jews. In 1838, the government was compelled to revoke many of the freedoms given to Jews earlier.

However, during the last half of the 19th century, most legislative disabilities that targeted Jews were repealed, and in 1910, the Swedish Riksdag passed an act granting Jews equality before the law. By that time, about 4,000 Jews lived in the country. This number increased rapidly to almost 7,000 by the 1920s following the influx of Jewish refugees running from virulent anti-Semitism and pogroms in Russia and Poland.

Neutral Sweden during World War II

During the 1930s, some 3,000 Jews migrated to Sweden fleeing Nazi persecution. At the same time, the Swedish government allowed German companies to fire Jewish employees and then gave free passage to the Nazis marching into Norway. Also, like in most other countries, including the United States, Swedish immigration policy was restrictive against admitting a high number of Jewish refugees. However, after the deportation of Norwegian Jews began, Sweden turned into a true safe haven for the Scandinavian Jewry. In 1942, 900 Norwegian Jews (about 40 percent of the Norwegian Jewish population) were given asylum, and in October 1943, almost the entire Danish Jewish community of close to 8,000 people was transported to Sweden in fishing boats. As part of the official Swedish policy, Raoul Wallenberg, a Swedish diplomat in Budapest, heroically saved thousands of Hungarian Jews by providing them with Swedish "protective passports." During the last few weeks of the war, the Swedish Red Cross undertook a program, known as the White Buses that rescued concentration camp inmates who came from the Scandinavian countries. After negotiations led by Count Folke Bernadotte, some 15,000 inmates were saved in the last months of the war, including 423 Danish Jews. In addition to the White Buses, a Swedish train brought to safety some 2,000 female inmates, including 960 Jewish women that were later transported to Copenhagen, Denmark, and Malmo, Sweden.

Sweden – present

"I have two sons, and I have to choose between giving them a strong, positive Jewish identity and keeping them safe, and I don't see that as a choice that we should have to make." Annika Hernroth-Rothstein, a Swedish writer and activist for Israel who fights against anti-Semitism, in an interview with Swedish Radio, November 2013.

My husband and I struggled to reconcile our idea of Sweden as a safe haven for Jews with the number of disturbing reports we encountered on the current situation in Malmo where violent Jew-hatred ran rampant. How do we interpret, I thought, Annika Hernroth-Rothstein asking for political asylum in her own country to attract the world's attention to growing anti-Semitism there?

I emailed my question, "How does one live as a Jew in today's Sweden?" to Mr. John Gradowski, the Head of Information and Public Relations for the Jewish Community of Stockholm. John graciously agreed to meet with us and share his opinion of the current situation.

Understanding Jewish Sweden with John Gradowski

John met us at the entrance to the Great Synagogue, located on Wahrendorffsgatan Street, in the heart of Stockholm called Norrmalm, close to the beautiful Kungstradgarden Park, which indeed as its name suggests, used to be a King's garden. Designated as a National Historic site, the Synagogue is an impressive building designed by renowned architect Frederik Wilhel Scholander in the 1860s. We followed John to the Holocaust memorial, inaugurated by King Carl XVI Gustaf of Sweden in 1998. The memorial is a 42-meter wall leading from the Synagogue's entrance to the Jewish Community office building. Names of 8,500 victims, relatives of the Jews of Sweden, are engraved on this wall, serving as a link between "a monstrous past and a future in which such atrocities should not be repeated," said John. In the synagogue yard, he pointed to a sculpture of an elderly Jewish man rushing away with a Torah in his hands. Called "Flight with a Torah," it was made by Russian-born Swedish Jewish artist Willy Gordon as a memorial to Sweden being a safe haven during the Holocaust.

When we entered the Synagogue's beautiful sanctuary, John Gradowski gave us an overview of the Jewish community. In the post-war period, many Jewish refugees from the Baltic Countries, Romania, and Poland immigrated to Sweden. Famous American cartoonist Art Spiegelman was born in Stockholm; his father Vladek Spiegelman settled there after surviving Auschwitz. More waves of refugees came from Hungary in 1956 and from Czechoslovakia in 1968 fleeing Communist governments. Between 1945 and 1970, the Jewish population of Sweden doubled. Today, however, there is no ethnic registration in Sweden, so the Jewish population can only be roughly estimated. According to the Official Council of Swedish Jewish Communities, that estimation is about 20,000. Compared to 1,400 Jews in Norway and 8,000 in Denmark, Sweden's Jewish community is the largest in Scandinavia. About 30 percent of Swedish Jews are affiliated with synagogues, which is highly remarkable since the Scandinavians in general are the most secular and the least church-going people in Europe. In addition to Stockholm, Malmo, Gothenburg, Boras, Helsingborg, Lund, and Uppsala, all have Jewish communities. Stockholm has the largest community of about 14,000 people, including 4,000 members that belong to any of the city's three synagogues. The community boasts a primary school, kindergarten, library, a bi-monthly publication (Judisk Kronika), and a weekly Jewish radio program. The Great Synagogue used to be Orthodox, but a members' referendum ten years ago decreed a mixed sitting, and now the services here are egalitarian conservative.

John told us about the non-Jewish visitors regularly coming to Shabbat services or to the Synagogue's study group. The non-Jewish students are, surprisingly, mostly women, a "gentile cultural elite," John called them. We asked John about the relationships with Chabad, since we were under the impression from talking to other Swedish Jews, that Chabad's arrival in 2001 made many of them nervous and anxious that their liberal traditions and relationship with non-Jewish Swedes might be jeopardized by Chabad's more traditional values. "Not at all," said John, explaining that as long as Chabad does not preach their own views while in the Synagogues, they are very welcome to the services and events. "Chabad is another religious and cultural offering for Swedish Jews," explained John.

Chabad's Shabbat dinners are often attended by over one hundred people, most of them young.

We discussed the much publicized rise of anti-Semitism in Sweden and Annika Hernroth-Rothstein's stand for preserving Jewish identity. I read aloud the excerpts from her articles and asked John to comment. "I know that the only way to survive as a Jew in my country is not to be seen as one," Hernroth-Rothstein wrote in the August 2013 issue of *Mosaic* journal. She took a firm stand against the Swedish government's outlawing circumcision and kosher cattle slaughter (banned since 1937). "What frightens me most is that my government is proscribing Jewish life," concluded Hernroth-Rothstein. "By outlawing circumcision, banning kosher slaughter, and telling us forthrightly that the only way to avoid being harassed in the streets is to distance ourselves from Israel, they are reinventing the conditions of the Eastern Europe[an] past that brought our community to this country in the first place." In November 2013, Hernroth-Rothstein undertook a publicity event when she filed for political asylum in her own country. A third-generation citizen in the country that prides itself on being a model of diversity and openness, Hernroth-Rothstein cited "well-founded" reasons to fear living as a Jew in Sweden. It seems that Hernroth-Rothstein and her friends are very much familiar with such fears. In Stockholm, she led "kippah walks"—marches by Jews and non-Jews who wore yarmulkes or kippahs (scalp caps) as a protest against anti-Semitism. Unfortunately, I was not able to talk to Hernroth-Rothstein: she chose not to return my calls.

When John Gradowski commented that he could neither agree nor support her views, I cited the CFCA (Coordination Forum for Countering Anti-Semitism) and Moshe Kantor (the President of the European Jewish Congress). The CFSA states that anti-Semitism in Sweden nowadays focuses on the Israeli-Palestinian conflict, while quoting Mr. Kantor that the only European country refusing to discuss the problem of anti-Semitism prevailing within its borders is Sweden. John explained that Swedish democrats in the government do support Israel in general but they do not approve of those traditions that are foreign to the Swedish understanding of what is "civilized" and "humane." For example, circumcision is seen as a violation of children's rights. John also told us that he was convinced that anti-Semitism in Sweden is endemic to only some, still holding on to their old-world anger, elements within the new immigrant communities.

We asked John Gradowski to share his view on the situation in Malmo, a southern Swedish city whose population of about 300,000 includes a few thousand Jews and 100,000 residents who emigrated from various Middle Eastern and African countries. Over the last few years, the atmosphere of anti-Semitic hostility and violence has become especially acute for the Jews who live there. Molotov cocktails were thrown inside and outside a funeral chapel at an old Jewish cemetery. In 2013, Malmo saw 60 anti-Semitic attacks, some vicious and violent, which accounted for 40 percent of anti-Semitic hate crimes documented in Sweden, according to the Swedish National Council for Crime Prevention. The international United Nations Watch organization that discussed the anti-Semitic attacks in Malmo in relation to Sweden's candidacy for membership in the UN Human Rights Council called on Sweden to supply adequate protection for the Jewish community and to develop initiatives aimed at educating against anti-Semitism.

The perpetrators, explained John, belonged to a small group of poorly-educated, non-assimilated individuals who were irritated by the fact that a then Chabad Rabbi was wearing his typical clothes around the city. In addition, Malmo used to have a controversial mayor who did not take adequate care of the situation and made some derogatory remarks in regards to the Jewish population and Israel. Currently, the Rabbi is gone, there is a new mayor, and the situation is improving. "You see," said John, "there are two tracks: one leads to embracing our values of diversity, inclusion, and appreciation of each other's differences, while another is still a circle of old anger and prejudices. But eventually, there will be only the first track and people who came to live in Sweden will adopt Sweden's world outlook." When we were leaving, John advised us to see the Raol Wallenberg memorial in the park nearby.

Thinking of Raol Wallenberg in Stockholm

Raol Wallenberg's monument was designed by Danish sculptor Kirsten Ortwed in 2002 and is known as one of the most controversial Holocaust memorials. Placed in the park near the Baltic Sea, the memorial is a granite globe with an engraved sentence circling it multiple times, first in Swedish, then in English, followed by 22 languages, representing the victims' native languages, beginning with Polish, the language of the largest group. The text reads: "The road was straight, when Jews were deported to death. The road was winding, dangerous and full of obstacles, when Jews were trying to escape from the murderers." Most in Stockholm found this sculpture almost meaningless due to its abstract form and lack of adequate expression. We could not help but think that this sculpture expressed an unsatisfactory language of commemoration.

Standing by the monument, we pondered the tragic fate of Raol Wallenberg, a hero venerated in the United States, Israel, Hungary, and several other countries for his rescue mission and eventual disappearance into the Soviet Gulag. However, Wallenberg was never given strong recognition in his native country. I heard various reasons for this, such as that some branches of his family were involved in banking and had dealings with the Germans; his mission was murky, a curious mixture of Swedish diplomacy dealing with the American War Refugee Board; and that he arrived in Budapest too late, in July 1944, by which time approximately 400,000 Hungarian Jews had already been deported ... Gently touching Wallenberg's name on the granite globe, I thought that we may probably never know how many lives he actually saved. What we do know is Wallenberg's heroic courage and passionate commitment to life. He chose to help the Jews when most turned away. He was one extraordinary man who made a difference. The mystery of his disappearance in the Soviet prisons remains unsolved. Since the fall of the Soviet Union, two official joint investigations, Swedish and Russian, failed to provide any answers. What were the circumstances and cause for his arrest? Why he was not released together with his Swedish colleagues? The unexplained indifference of the Swedish government during the first crucial years of Wallenberg's disappearance is nothing short of a (intentional?) diplomatic blunder that Sweden, two generations later, has yet to explore.

Meeting Ira Vlasova, a Moscow-born Israeli and a Stockholm Jew

We left Wallenberg torg (square) and went to Stockholm City Hall, the venue of the Nobel Prize annual banquet. The seat of the

Municipal Council for the City, this impressive building was designed in the National Romanticism style. Its spire is topped by three golden crowns, and it is one of the most famous silhouettes in Stockholm. There, we met Ira Vlasova, our guide. A vivacious and enthusiastic young woman with a talent for bringing history to life, Ira exemplifies young secular Stockholm with all its 21st-century diversity and optimistic faith in a bright future. When we talked about young Jews in Sweden, Ira, who has been living in Stockholm for over 10 years, told us about her diverse group of friends: Swedes, Jews with either European or Israeli backgrounds, and Muslims; all, she said, are Swedish first and foremost. Sometimes, she said, her Palestinian friends would tease her by showing her a map of the Middle East without the State of Israel. She immediately would take her marker and draw the outlines of the country where she spent the first 10 years of her life after emigrating there with her parents from Moscow when she was a baby. "We just laugh," she said. "And agree to disagree. Then go dancing." Ira was not aware of the anti-Semitic violence in Malmo; this was not her Sweden. "In the country I know and love," she told us, "we all believe in respecting each other, in acceptance and equality, no matter what your religion or political outlooks are. Eventually all serious disagreements would be resolved. This is what Sweden is all about." At the end of our conversation, Ira mentioned Paideia, a "secular yeshiva," as she called this organization, where some of her friends, some Jewish, some not, are working. "Only in Sweden," she said.

A secular, cultural vision of Jewish life

Paideia, the European Institute for Jewish Studies in Sweden, is a non-denominational academic entity that was established in 2000 with funding provided by the Swedish government. The name, Paideia, in ancient Greek refers to the rearing and education of ideal citizens. Swedish Paideia is dedicated to the revival of Jewish culture in Europe. Its mission is to educate intellectual leaders of Europe so that they become familiar with the Jewish textual sources that have served as the wellsprings of the Jewish civilization. In renewing interpretation of the Jewish text, Paideia's vision is to revive a European Jewish voice long silenced by Communism and post-

Holocaust trauma, a voice that can contribute to a culturally rich and pluralistic Europe.

A complicated Jewish story

In 2013, The Forward newspaper quoted Charles Small, director of the Yale Initiative for the Study of Anti-Semitism: "Sweden is a microcosm of contemporary anti-Semitism," Small stated. "It's a form of acquiescence to radical Islam, which is diametrically opposed to everything Sweden stands for." For us that was an image of Sweden-Malmo with its violence and hostility, not fully resolved even today. Adding to this image, Annika Hernroth-Rothstein and her circle embody the situation where human rights and religious traditions are jeopardized behind the sharp criticism of Israel and the mask of cowardly cultural relativism. On the other hand, my understanding of the official position of the Jewish Community of Stockholm, as expressed by its Head of Information, John Gradowski, is that based on the belief that if current incidents are not elevated to a crisis level and exasperated by too much "Jewishness," then Swedish values of democracy and pluralism would be eventually embraced by everyone who chooses to call Sweden home. At the same time, young Jews like Ira Vlasova illustrate a unique and vibrant secularism of Swedish life, where its citizens fiercely guard their liberal traditions.

By the end of our visit to Sweden, this country's Jewish narrative proved to be a puzzle of a multitude of voices and views. The last destination on our Scandinavian journey was Denmark.

Selected Sources

Lindqvist, H. A History of Sweden. Norstedts Forlag, 2006.

Booth, M. The Almost Nearly Perfect People: Behind the Myth of the Scandinavian Utopia. Picador, NY, 2014

"Sweden—the New Center of Anti-Semitism." Coordination Forum for Countering Anti-Semitism, 2013

"Anti-Semitism in Malmo Reaches New, Horrific Depths," Simon Wiesenthal Center, March 2015.

Slussen (The Locks) in Stockholm. The bridge over the canal separates the fresh water of Lake Malaren and salt water of the Baltic Sea.

The Stockholm Concert Hall with Carl Milles's statue "Orpheus Emerging from the Underworld." Home of the annual Nobel Prize award ceremony.

The Stockholm Stadshuset or the City Hall (1923) is built in the
North National Romantic style (similar to British Arts & Crafts).

The renowned Blue Hall in the Stockholm City Hall where the
Nobel Prize winners' banquet takes place.

The Great Synagogue of Sweden (1860) is located in Stockholm.

The Great Synagogue interior.

The Wall of Names in the Stockholm Synagogue courtyard. These are the 8,500 names of Swedish Jewish citizens' relatives who perished in the Holocaust.

The "Flight with a Torah" sculpture in the Stockholm Synagogue courtyard was made by Russian-born Swedish Jewish artist Willy Gordon.

These stones, displayed in the Stockholm Synagogue courtyard, were brought from the Budapest Ghetto. The rails carried the deportation trains to Auschwitz.

The author with Mr. John Gradowski, Head of Information for the Stockholm Jewish Community. The Great Synagogue, Stockholm.

Raul Wallenberg memorial in Stockholm, designed by Danish sculptor Kirsten Ortwed in 2002.

The Raul Wallenberg memorial in Stockholm is one of the most controversial Holocaust monuments in Europe.

Conversation about young, secular Sweden. The author with Ira Vlasova in the Blue Hall of the City Hall in Stockholm.

View on the Paidea from the canal in Stockholm. Paidea is the European Institute for Jewish Studies in Sweden.

Nyhavn or New Harbor, is the 17th-century waterfront in
Copenhagen.

Anti-Semitism and Violence in the Righteous among the Nations

In our attempt to understand the complex realities of the Scandinavian Jewish story, we had traveled through Norway and Sweden and continued on to our next destination, Denmark. After all, this was the only country in the world that defied Hitler and saved its Jewish community almost in its entirety. I wanted to solve what I called my "Danish Paradox": how did it happen that Denmark, a heroic exception in the history of the Holocaust, is becoming, as expressed by Italian journalist Giulio Meotti, a "bit of an exception once again, in Europe's post-Holocaust anti-Semitism?"

In retrospect, reflecting now on our May 2014 visit, our meetings, and conversations that took place in all three Scandinavian capitals, it seems that the February 2015 violence in Copenhagen, and an overall hostile anti-Semitic atmosphere in this country, were not as unexpected and shocking.

Denmark – past

"It's Hard to be a Jew." The title of Sholem Aleichem's play written in Copenhagen in 1914.

Denmark became the first of the Scandinavian countries where Jews were permitted to settle. In 1622, the Renaissance Danish King Christian IV, ever a pragmatist, sent a message to the Sephardic (or as they were called in Denmark, "Portuguese") Jews of Amsterdam and Hamburg inviting them to come to his kingdom and settle, not in his capital of course, but in the newly established town of Glukstadt. The king had his Mint there but no mintmaster. The Jews came, and quickly succeeded in everything they were permitted to do, from running the Royal Mint, to trading and manufacturing, to finance and jewelry-making. As documented in the Royal Archives, Benjamin Mussafa was a physician to the royal family in 1646. His son-in-law rose to become a governor of the Danish West Indies in 1684 (alas, arrested and convicted few years later for misappropriation of funds). In Denmark, unlike any other European country, rabbis were permitted to openly practice and teach Judaism in their communities. Following the costly Thirty Years' War (1618-1648), Frederik III encouraged larger Jewish immigration into his realm to improve his international trade status. By 1780, there were approximately 1,600 Jews in Denmark, though all were admitted on the basis of personal wealth. But the Jews of Denmark were not required to live in ghettos and had a significant degree of self-governance. In the late 18th century, the king instituted a number of reforms, and Jews were allowed to join guilds, study at the university, buy real estate, and establish schools. The Napoleonic Wars brought about a complete emancipation of Danish Jews.

The 19th century saw a flourishing of Danish-Jewish cultural life. The Great Synagogue of Copenhagen was built, designed by the renowned architect G. F. Hetsch. A number of Jewish cultural personalities rose to prominence. Among them were art benefactor and collector Mendel Levin Nathanson, popular writer Meir Aron Goldschmidt, and literary critic Georg Brandes, who had a strong influence on Norwegian playwright Henrik Ibsen. In the outbreak of World War I, the great Jewish Yiddish writer Sholem Aleichem and his family found refuge in Denmark fleeing violent anti-Semitism in Russia and Ukraine. In Copenhagen, Sholem Aleichem began writing his tragicomedy *It's Hard to be a Jew*. While enjoying an open and inclusive atmosphere in the Danish capital city, the Jewish writer, with his typical sardonic irony, placed the action of this play in "a City in Czarist Russia where Jews were not permitted to reside." Denmark proved to be a different story.

Denmark during World War II: rescue of the Danish Jews

In 1933, the year Hitler came to power in Germany, Christian X of Denmark became the first Scandinavian monarch to visit a synagogue. He wanted to honor the centennial anniversary of the Great Synagogue of Copenhagen. Christian X became the subject of a persistent legend saying that he had the yellow Star of David sewn on his clothes and wore them in the streets of Copenhagen during the Nazi occupation. That never really happened, and the Danish Jews were not required to wear yellow stars. But this is how Christian X, who personally financed the secret transport of his kingdom's Jews to safety into a neutral Sweden, is forever remembered in history.

Nazi occupation of Denmark was relatively mild for the first three years (1940-43), at least comparing to other European countries. The Germans even referred to Denmark as "the model protectorate." The King retained his throne, and the Rigsdag (parliament) continued to function. The Danish government persistently stated that there was no "Jewish problem" in their country.

However, by the end of the summer in 1943, the tide of war turned. The Nazis lost under Stalingrad, their attack at Kursk failed, the Allies landed in Sicily, and Hamburg was bombed by the U.S. and British air forces. The Danish Resistance forces, anticipating the war's end, increased their activities, and German policies in Denmark sharply changed. In August 1943, the Nazis arrested 100 prominent Danes. In response, the Danish government resigned, the Nazis took over and immediately began planning the deportation of Danish Jews. A German diplomat Georg Duckwitz, who is now commemorated in Israel's Yad Vashem as a Righteous Gentile, secretly tried to reach an agreement with Sweden to create a safe place there to harbor Danish Jews. When the Swedes responded that they needed the Nazis' approval, Niels Bohr, the world-famous Danish physicist and a Jew, made a personal appeal for his countrymen to the Swedish King. Bohr was hiding in Sweden at that time on his way to the United States to work on the Manhattan Project. Bohr refused to go to the U.S. until the "Jewish question" was decided by the Swedish government. Whether Bohr did play a pivotal role in Sweden making their decision or not, in October 1943, Sweden agreed to shelter the entire Danish Jewish community, and close to 8,000 people were smuggled out of Denmark over the Oresund strait to Sweden. One of the fishing boats that transported Danish Jews to freedom is exhibited in the United States Holocaust Museum in Washington D.C. and another in Yad Vashem in Israel. There, Denmark is honored as the "Righteous among the Nations" for unprecedented heroism and selfless good will.

There were numerous possible explanations given by European historians of why the Danes behaved drastically different from all other nations in relation to their Jewish compatriots. The rescue operation was very easy logistically, since the Jewish population was so small and most Jews lived in and near Copenhagen. Jews were so strongly integrated into Danish society that the Danes did not see them as the "others." The importance of a small, close-knit community was an integral part of Danish national consciousness. Whatever the reasons, the Danes as one nation stood up against evil when the rest of the world turned away.

However, our visit to Denmark was focused on not so much a historic study but an understanding of the present. I called the Great Synagogue in Copenhagen and was connected to their Chief Cantor, Mr. Oren Atzmor. After I stated the reason for my call and the "Danish Paradox" question that bothered me a great deal, Mr. Atzmor said: "Nothing is straightforward. Let's talk."

Denmark – present

"One of the world's most attractive nations for immigrants and tourists alike has become a very dangerous place for the Jews." Giulio Meotti, Exposed: Denmark Unsafe for Jews. Arutz Sheva, Israeli National News, May 2013.

As a curious historic coincidence, the main synagogue in Copenhagen is located in close proximity to major historical landmarks of the Danish capital, including the royal Rosenborg Palace and the observatory called Round Tower, both representing favorite building projects of King Christian IV, who was the first Scandinavian ruler to open his country to Jews. During the Nazi occupation, the Torah scrolls of the synagogue were hidden at the Trinitatis Church, right next to the Round Tower. After marveling at the Hebrew lettering on the Round Tower that, as we were told, signified the name of God, we went to Krystalgade Street where Mr. Oren Atzmor waited for us at the synagogue.

Conversations with the Chief Cantor of the Great Synagogue of Copenhagen

Cantor Oren gave us a brief tour of this magnificent building where he and the Chief Rabbi work and live. The synagogue building, the Cantor explained, is one of the very few of its period (1830s) to abandon the classical tradition. The famous architect G. F. Hetsch used Egyptian elements in the columns; his design was defined by the building's unique architecture around the Ark of the Law with Egyptian motifs on the ceiling and cornice over the Ark itself. Perhaps the architect, a non-Jew, wanted to emphasize that the Exodus from Egypt was a defining episode in forming the Jewish identity, I said. "Or," replied Cantor Oren, "perhaps he just preferred pseudo-Oriental style over Greek or Roman." "Nothing is straightforward here," he repeated. The Cantor planned to start our visit in the main sanctuary, but on that weekday morning, the sanctuary was occupied by a study group of about 30 to 40 people who had their Jewish history class. All of them are non-Jews, said Cantor Oren. Registering our surprised faces, he explained, "Non-Jewish Danes take a growing interest in Judaism. Some even come to the services on a regular basis." Cantor invited us to talk in the conference room first and visit the sanctuary when the class is over.

Cantor Oren Atzmor is a true citizen of the world. An Israeli by birth, he was educated as an opera singer in Vienna and as a wind instrument player in Berlin. Over twenty years ago, a friend from Copenhagen invited Oren to come from Vienna and interview for the job of the Chief Cantor, the position he has held ever since. Oren Atzmor is a typical European intellectual with a profound knowledge of literature, theater, and of course, music. Learning about our Russian origin, Oren beautifully sang an aria from *Prince Igor.*

"My Master Thesis," he explained, effortlessly changing from the operatic part to that of a cantor in a major synagogue, Oren continued with the Danish Jewish story.

There are about 7,000-8,000 Jews living in Denmark today, with less than one percent of them residing in Odense and Aarhus. Approximately 2,000 people belong to the Great Synagogue and about 1,000 belong to the other three much smaller congregations. This vibrant community supports an active Zionist Federation, Women's International Zionist organization, B'nai B'rith, Jewish school, and several publications, with Joedisk Orientering being the leading Jewish magazine in the country. Almost all the Jews who were rescued during the war returned back home, but the birth rate is low and the numbers keep diminishing. I shared the main reason for our visit, my "Danish Paradox" question, with Oren and asked him to share his perspective.

In January 2013, seventeen-year old Moran Jacob testified at a Copenhagen City Hall hearing on growing anti-Semitism in the Danish capital and described the harassment he experienced for years while living in Norrebro, a heavily Muslim neighborhood of his home town. His testimony was corroborated by Max Mayer, the President of the Danish Zionist Federation, who stated that "Danish Jews learned to keep a low profile in the city: "To pretend not to exist" (Front Page Magazine, October 1, 2013). I had clippings from various publications stating that the Danish Jewish community documented 40 violent anti-Semitic incidents in 2013, almost double compared to 2009. Some journalists traced the beginning of open anti-Semitic hatred to 2001, when an anonymous poster in Arabic was pinned to the bulletin board in one of the colleges in Copenhagen. The poster promised $35,000 to anyone who would kill a Jew. An Italian journalist, Giulio Meotti, wrote that it is just as unsafe in 2013 to be a Jew in Copenhagen as it is to be a Jew in most Middle-Eastern countries.

"Yes," agreed Cantor Oren, "barbed-wire and security guards surround the Jewish school in Copenhagen. And yes, there are 'no-go' neighborhoods in our city. That would be highly unusual 10 years or so ago." Some young people from his congregation are either planning to leave Denmark or have already left for Israel, the United States, or Australia. But this "situation" (Orin emphasized the quote signs) "should not be exaggerated and elevated to an emergency crisis level." "This is no more than a temporary issue," he insisted, "and the best way to deal with it now is to ignore it." "Ignore it?" I thought I misunderstood our new friend. "Oh, yes," he said. He then proceeded to tell us about his recent experience that he thought was rather humorous.

While going shopping at one of the exclusive department stores, Cantor Oren was confronted at the store entrance by a group of young Middle-Eastern men. "Are you Jewish?" they angrily asked. "From Israel?" Oren, who, as an undergrad, majored in Arabic studies in Tel-Aviv, confirmed in pure Arabic that he indeed was from Israel but that he was an Arab. Enjoying this role-playing, Oren recited a verse from the Koran right in front of the perplexed youths, "There is no God but Allah…" "They left," said Oren. We were impressed but not amused. "Listen," I said, "what if you happen to be a non-Arabic-major regular Jewish guy, what then?" Our new friend smiled: "Oh, I might've been beat up."

Otherwise, Oren did not experience any harassment and did not know personally anyone who did. The issue of kosher slaughter being outlawed in Denmark, just like in Sweden or Norway, did not bother him at all. "I am a vegetarian anyway," he said. His personal concern had more to do with the inability of a "foreigner" to become accepted by the Danish Jewish community, even if this foreigner was invited to serve as a Chief Cantor for the Great Synagogue of Copenhagen. So, another of Oren's stories was of royalty, Jewish royalty, to be precise. "I am not a Dane so [I am] able to present an outsider's perspective," he said. Oren Atzmor sees the Jewish community of Copenhagen as a parallel reality to the gentile society of Denmark with its profound respect and admiration for their royal family, one of the oldest continuous monarchies in the world. The Danish Jews have their own royalty, the Melhiors, whose ancestor was one of the first Jews invited by King Christian IV to settle in Denmark. "This is our reigning dynasty," said the Cantor. "The rabbis of the Great Synagogue and the decision-making Board, all have to come from or be closely-related to the family. Otherwise you are not really an "in-person." Oren did not think that his twenty-plus years among the clergy of the largest Danish congregation made him less of an outsider.

Our new friend, both a citizen of Denmark and a citizen-of-the-world, polyglot and erudite, a dedicated Jewish clergy and a passionate European musician, left us with more disturbing questions than definitive answers. But we were not done with Denmark's Jewish narrative. We headed to the Jewish Museum.

Reflecting on architecture telling the story: The Jewish Museum of Denmark

Located within both an historic and contemporary architectural complex (the Renaissance Royal Boat House—turned the Nordic

Romantic Royal Library—turned Post-Modern Black Diamond building), the museum tells its story even before you enter. In the seventeenth century, King Christian IV built his Royal Boat House, which was renovated in the early 1900s to become a part of the adjacent Royal Library. At the end of the twentieth century, the Black Diamond building, nicknamed for its shiny black glass walls, designed to serve as a cultural center and an exhibition space, connected both the old and new libraries and instantly became one of the most beloved landmarks of contemporary Copenhagen. In the 1990s, the Society for Danish Jewish History hired world-renowned Polish-American architect Daniel Libeskind to create the Danish Jewish Museum. Libeskind thought the complex that consists of the Royal Boat House turned into a Library and the Black Diamond building contained a unique intellectual context in which the Danish Jewish Museum would represent a deep historical legacy. In June 2004, one of the most unusual of museums opened its doors.

The architect designed the museum's layout to incorporate a pedestrian walk between the new and old libraries, outdoor summer seating for a café, and intimate conversation spaces at the ground level near the entrance. When we entered the exhibition itself, we found ourselves inside a...Word. This word is in Hebrew: *Mitzvah*, meaning "good deed." It is best to start with an introductory movie before venturing ahead. This was where we learned about not only the Jewish history of Denmark but also about the architect's way of immortalizing it in his design. In the movie, Libeskind explains: "The Danish Jewish Museum will become a destination which will reveal the deep tradition and its future in the ...space of Mitzvah... a dynamic dialogue between architecture of the past and of the future - the newness of the old and the agelessness of the new. The Danish Jewish Museum differs from all other European Jewish Museums because Danish Jews were, by and large, saved through the effort of their compatriots and neighbors during the tragic years of the Shoa. It is this deeply human response that differentiates the Danish Jewish community and is manifested in the form, structure and light of the new museum. Mitzvah is the guiding light of this project."

And indeed, the entire exhibition space is full of light coming through stained glass windows. Libeskind wanted us to feel "a microcosm of Mitzvah transforming light across the day." The architect organized the building inside as a series of planes, each corresponding to a particular field of historic and religious narrative: Exodus, Wilderness, The Giving of the Law, and The Promised Land. Interior corridors consist of fractured passageways and slanted floors. This is how the corridors, which serve as the museum's exhibition spaces, whirl us around and form the Hebrew letters for the word Mitzvah. As the museum's website states, the form of the building becomes a commentary on the artifacts it presents, paralleling how accompanying texts often illuminate different aspects of the Talmud. Libeskind describes the space as a "sort of text running within a frame made up of many other surfaces—walls, inner spaces, showcases, virtual perspectives." A visitor literally walks inside the four huge Hebrew letters, a landscape both enigmatic and expressive. Guided by the architect's genius and the uniqueness of the Danish Jewish narrative, we were able to create our own experience, at once deeply memorable and highly personal.

A chat at the Jewish Museum: the flag of Israel as a provocation

When we were leaving the museum it was closing, but a few young women working at the cloak room and the bookstore kindly agreed to chat with us. We felt overwhelmed by the museum experience and wanted to share our feelings. However, the conversation turned to today's Denmark and the growing tensions between the Jewish and the new immigrant communities. One girl shared how she, a year or so ago, participated in the "Taste the World" festival as a member of the Danish Zionist Federation (DZF). The festival was supposed to demonstrate the diversity and inclusiveness of Denmark and to feature the foods and cultures of various nations living in Copenhagen. The city council, however, believed that the DZF displaying Israeli food would be a mistake. The DZF decided to participate anyway, and the council requested they would not display the Israeli flag. "Taste the World" was held in Norrebro, a large borough home to the city's North African, Middle Eastern, and Balkan immigrants. The DZF were the only vendors without the flag identifying the food products' origin. The council believed that an Israeli flag might be a provocation, but to display all other flags was OK.

Scandinavian sense of history – European style

"Despite their image of moral innocence and best intentions, the lands of the north have become home to a scary, new form of anti-Semitism." Liam Hoare, The Scandal of Scandinavia, *The Tower* (U.K.), April 2013

At the completion of our travel through Norway, Sweden, and Denmark, we reflected on these three Scandinavian countries' sense of history and current realities.

Unlike the majority of American Jews, the Jews of Scandinavia and indeed of most of Europe are largely children and grandchildren of Holocaust survivors or (very few now) survivors themselves. A smaller percentage of European Jews were expelled from North African or Middle Eastern countries during the second half of the last century. Most European Jews know all too well, from either personal experiences or inherited knowledge, how a normal, secure, and comfortable life can be destroyed overnight. So, perhaps, this is why when they see anti-Semitic incidents rising, some cannot help but feel that history is getting ready to repeat itself. At the same time, there is a prevalent attempt to dismiss these incidents as a non-entity. A renowned Danish journalist and a TV personality Martin Krasnik is quoted in "Hiding Judaism in Copenhagen:" "Anti-Semitism is strictly endemic to only new immigrant neighborhoods. It's the same in London, it's the same in Paris" (Michael Moynihan, *Tablet*, March 2013). Anti-Jewish sentiment is virtually unknown in Denmark, so what's happening is a "small shift imported from the Middle East," insists Krasnik.

Norwegian Jo Nesbo, one of the most popular crime fiction writers in Europe, stated that Norwegians, as indeed most Scandinavians, are "in love with their restrained response to tragedy or violence," considering themselves "so calm, wise, and full of love." As history shows, Scandinavians have been much more accepting and respectful of "others" and much less traditionally anti-Semitic than other Europeans. In his piece "The Scandinavian Scandal," U.K. journalist Liam Haare states, "the problem today is not widespread traditional anti-Semitism but rather a new kind of hate, derived mainly from the failure to distinguish between Israel, Zionism, and local Jewish communities in political discourse… anti-Zionism has rechanneled anti-Semitism." As he and other journalists point out, this issue is especially acute in small Scandinavian countries, where Jews, who are the smallest of minorities but well-integrated into their home countries live in close proximity to much larger and non-integrated immigrant communities from North Africa and the Middle East that often display extremist anti-Israel and anti-Jewish feelings.

Shall we hope then, as John Gradowski, the Head of Information for the Jewish Community of Stockholm suggested, for the "first track?" By that Mr. Gradowski meant the socio-economic way of new immigrants' development toward accepting the openness and inclusiveness of Swedish values.

Indeed, all Scandinavian countries, the least church going and the most secular in Europe, made Jewish studies and Holocaust education a way to open up minds and increase awareness. Non-Jews come to synagogues and museums to learn about Judaism. Schools bring their students to Holocaust and Jewish history museums as an integral part of their curriculums. At the same time, certain cultural attitudes, such as animal or children rights, led to governments' prohibition of kosher slaughter and circumcision, which for some observant Jews are nothing short of anti-Semitic acts since they touch on central traditions of Jewish life. Given the demographic changes with the fast-growing new immigrant communities and the current intensity of anti-Israel campaigns throughout Europe, could all these trends promote a disturbing sense of "otherness" toward the Jews?

The same "otherness" that encourages seeing the Jews, with their connection to a foreign state and their "strange" traditions, as markedly and conspicuously different from everybody else and less acceptable because of it? Then, it would not matter how much the Jews contributed to or how well they were integrated into their home-countries' gentile societies.

Selected Sources

Berman, L. "Swedish Jew Files for Asylum in Her own Country," The Times of Israel, September 2013.

Hoare, L. "The Scandal of Scandinavia," The Tower, April 2103.

Jespersen, K. J. V. A History of Denmark. Second Edition. Palgrave Macmillan, 2011.

Krasnik, M. "Hiding Judaism in Copenhagen," Tablet, March 2013.

Red roofs of old Copenhagen.

Kronborg castle in Helsingor is the fictional home of the most
famous Danish royal, Prince Hamlet.

The Great Old Dane, who "lives" in the basement of the Kronborg castle. He wakes up when a catastrophe strikes his homeland.

The Great Synagogue of Copenhagen (1830). The February 2015 shootings took place here.

Interior of the Great Synagogue of Copenhagen. Danish architect
G. F. Hetch used Egyptian elements in his design.

The Holocaust Memorial in the courtyard of the Great Synagogue
of Copenhagen.

The author with Chief Cantor Oren Atzmor in the Great
Synagogue of Copenhagen.

Former Royal Boat House and Library transformed into the Jewish
Museum of Denmark by renowned architect Daniel Libeskind.

Entrance to the Jewish Museum designed by Libeskind as a Hebrew word Mitzvah, meaning a good deed.

Inside the Jewish Museum, the interior corridors form the Hebrew letters for the word Mitzvah and serve as the exhibition spaces.

Palermo Cathedral embraced the best of architectural styles of medieval Sicily: Romanesque, Arab, Norman, and Byzantine.

CHAPTER 8: PALERMO, SICILY

The Gateway to the Sicilian Jewish Story
With Bianca Del Bello*

"We, with the counsel and advice of prelates and great noblemen of our kingdoms... resolve to order the Jews and Jewesses of our kingdoms to depart and never to return or come back..." King Ferdinand and Queen Isabella of Spain, Edict of the Expulsion of the Jews, March 1492.

"The Anousim is a legal category of Jews in halakha who were forced to abandon Judaism against their will, while forcibly converted to another religion." Medieval Jewish History Resource Directory, 2014.

The Anousim led me to Sicily

Our many conversations that took place in Scandinavia and online correspondence with our friends in France often concluded with the same sad question: Is Europe finished for Jews once again?

I decided to return to my ongoing research on Italy, a country which had always been our sunny refuge for mind and body. Even after I saw the September 2015 issue of *The Times of Israel* with "Landmark Report Shows Italian Jewry Fearful of anti-Semitism," I still felt that if one European country was able to offer a ray of hope, this would be Italy. After all, this was where I found Rabbi Barbara and Bianca Del Bello, two people instrumental in opening up "the gates" to Sicily for me.

I came across Rabbi Barbara's name while researching the Jewish history of Italy. She is a woman of many "firsts:" first female and first non-Orthodox rabbi to head the first Reform synagogue in Italy. She is also the first leader, founder, and the force behind the new Italian Jewish movement, the *Anousim*. Rabbi Barbara Aiello was the first person to tell me about "the forced ones" from the south of Italy:

people who are rediscovering their Jewish roots and traditions many centuries after their ancestors were forcefully converted to Christianity. For many, as Rabbi Barbara said, this new knowledge leads to a new identity: formal conversion to Judaism.

During our phone and online conversations, Rabbi Barbara opened a door for me into the world of little-known Jewish history from the south of Italy. She talked about centuries marked by fear and secrets, decades filled with the search for one's identity, and courage to defy conventions and to reinvent oneself. All these were stories of the Anousim. This was how, in my quest for a global Jewish narrative, the islands of Sicily and Sardinia became my next destination. I was drawn to this world that emanated drama, secrecy, and defiance, the one I imagined from the Rabbi's stories. What I discovered in the process was a new understating of history and Jewish identity.

The stories of origin

The settlers

The Semitic people were the first group to colonize Sicily and establish a city-port they called Zis, now known as Palermo. They spoke a language similar to Hebrew and developed the first alphabet in the world that had less than thirty characters and was written like Hebrew, from right to left. The year was 800 BC and the people were Phoenicians, great sea traders from the Persian Gulf who settled many Mediterranean islands and established coastal cities. The Greeks came 100 years later; 500 years after the Greeks, the Romans arrived; 500 years after the Romans, the Vandals; then the Arabs, the Normans, the Schwabians, the French, and the Spanish. The last wave of invaders came after the unification of Italy in 1861. These were the "northern Italians," as the locals call them.

The name

In the aftermath of the Maccabees' rebellion against the Seleucid Greeks in the second century BC, Jewish scouting parties sailed from Judea in search of military alliances to assist them in their fight against their enemies. When the Jews approached the beautiful southern coastline of the Mediterranean, they supposedly exclaimed in admiration: "*Aiee tal ya*" or the "coast of God's dew." And this is how we have "Italia." No historical documents support this legend, but no evidence contradicts it either. And it makes for a good Jewish story, one of my most favorite that I heard from Rabbi Barbara.

My dear Palermian friend, Bianca Del Bello smiled when I told her that armed with the knowledge of these origin legends, we were ready for Sicily. Bianca is a beautiful Siciliana and European intellectual. A tour guide par excellence, she speaks several languages and is equally at home in any historical period of her ancient home city, Palermo. Only Bianca could turn five hours of sightseeing into an extensive experience of living and learning by traveling through three thousand years of Sicilian history.

From Bianca we learned that though Sicily (with its capital Palermo) geographically and administratively is indeed part of Italy, the Sicilians, culturally and linguistically, are not Italians. "We are the people of the most conquered island in the world, where one wave of invaders just changed another" said Bianca, "and so, we created and inhabited our own universe, where the past—Phoenician, Greek, Roman, Byzantine, Jewish, Arabic, Norman, French, and Spanish— was never rejected but accepted and embraced." The first logical stop to understand this unique world, she told us, was the Palermo Cathedral.

The Palermo Cathedral embraces "multiculturalism" of centuries

The Cathedral's immense eclectic structure is arguably the world's most architecturally diverse building. As we circled it, we pondered the meaning of "multiculturalism" and "inclusion," if these modern terms could be applied to an ancient place of worship. In architectural terms—certainly! The original church was built in the early medieval period on the site of a pagan temple, and many Punic or Phoenician ruins were still visible. Recently, the remains of a Roman temple have been excavated behind the Cathedral. Invading Saracen Arabs described this structure as an "infidel" building in 831 AD. It was of course converted into a mosque, the Great Mosque as it was called, and in a typical Sicilian fashion, no major structural changes were made. Then, in 1072, the Normans conquered the island, and the mosque was promptly reconsecrated as a Christian place of worship. By 1130, when Norman Count Roger was crowned as Roger I in this cathedral, the building probably still looked much like the mosque. Though the king was Christian, in the city, called either by its Greek name Panormus (Palermo) or the by its Arabic name Bal'harm, Muslims, Jews, and Christians—all enjoyed freedom of worship. The laws were published in several languages, including Hebrew, and on the streets one could hear Norman, Lombard, Greek, Arabic, Hebrew, and Sicilian speech as an amalgamation of them all. We saw an 11th-century funeral stone with inscriptions in four languages: Arabic, Greek, Hebrew, and Latin.

Under the Normans, Palermo became one of the wealthiest cities in Europe with revenue exceeding that of all of Plantagenet (Norman) England. During this period, an architectural miracle happened, and a uniquely Sicilian Norman-Arabic style was born. It embraced the best of all contemporary styles: Romanesque, Arab, Norman, and Byzantine. If other Sicilian cathedrals, for example in Monreale or Cefalu, are considered masterpieces of this style, it is the Palermo Cathedral that demonstrates the features of this style loudly and proudly as just another one of its "multicultural" adaptations. We slowly absorbed it all: the Byzantine icon of Madonna and Child over the entrance, the Moorish ornaments of the bell towers' double windows, the Arabic geometric inlays and stalactites-like decorations on the ceiling, the Catalan south porch, and the Aragonese coat-of-arms enhancing the middle portal. All these elements taken together were indeed the best introduction to Sicily and Sicilians. For only on this island, a paradise for any art lover, one can see and experience a successful harmonization of multiple diverse influences into a perfect work of art, be that mosaic or architecture, cuisine or gardening, or the country itself and its people. And the Jews of Sicily and its capital Palermo were fully integrated into this cosmopolitan, truly multicultural society until their forced exile from the island in 1492.

The oldest Jewish community in Europe was in Sicily

The records

During my conversations with Rabbi Barbara, she specifically emphasized the fact that, contrary to popular opinion, Sicily's Jewish culture was not imported from Spain but came from Judea in antiquity as part of the Diaspora. Some sources date the arrival of the first Jewish settlers in Sicily to the destruction of Jerusalem's Second Temple in 70 AD, when Titus brought over 30,000 Jewish slaves to Rome, some of whom were later sent to the island of Sicily. Academics generally agree, though, that the Jewish presence in Italy began long before that. It is recorded that in 161 BC, Judah Macabee, seeking military alliances, sent a delegation to the Roman Emperor. The Jews then settled in Trastevere, across the river from the center of Rome. Probably a few families of Jewish nobility also settled in Southern Italy at that time. It is also possible that a sizable Jewish community was established in the south-eastern part of Sicily in Siracusa during the Hellenistic Greek period, long before the Roman conquest of the island in the middle of the third century BC. Encyclopedia Judaica quotes the record of the first known European Jewish poet and rhetorician named Caecilius of Calacte who moved to Rome from Sicily in 50 AD, twenty years prior to Titus's slaves. What all these various records prove is that the Sicilian Jewish community is indeed the oldest in Europe.

The Pope and the Jews

The next known record that mentions the Jews of Sicily dates to 590 AD. It states that the Pope Gregory the Great sent a delegation to Palermo to resolve a dispute involving a large number of local Jews. At that time in Palermo, local priests tried to convert the Jews and confiscated one of the synagogues, so the Pope ordered them to return the property to its rightful owners and stop the coercion. A great story for the history of the Jewish-Catholic relationship! The story also reveals that in the 6th century AD, Palermian Jews were wealthy enough to become an attractive target for property appropriation and numerous enough to have more than one synagogue.

The Muslim rule

In 632 AD, Islam began to spread and by the end of the 7th century, about 90 percent of the world's Jews found themselves living in Islamic lands. When the Arabs conquered Sicily in 831, the Jewish community of Palermo was significantly larger due to a large number of Jews that came from Islamic countries. The new rulers required Sicilian Jews to pay special taxes and wear a distinctive badge, but they were considered the "People of the Book" and respected. At that time, there were flourishing Jewish communities in other Sicilian cities, such as Siracusa, Messina, Taormina, and Mazara among others. The Jews of Palermo conducted lucrative trade between Sicily, North Africa, and Egypt and prospered under Muslim rule. They spoke Arabic in addition to a Sicilian dialect and as historians note, their vernacular Hebrew was closer to Arabic than Yiddish was to German.

The Norman conquest

The Normans arrived in 1070 AD, and though the Jews still had to pay heavy taxes for their religion and wear a badge (a yellow cord required by the Arabs was changed to a small red wheel), the Jews were recognized as citizens and even allowed to hold public office and buy land. During the Norman period, travelers described the beauty of the Palermian synagogues and the wealth of the Jews. Benjamin of Tudela, himself a Jew, estimated that the 11th-century Palermian community numbered at least 1,500 families or close to 6,000 to 8,000 people. In addition to being successful merchants, the Jews of Palermo were physicians, money lenders, translators, and precious metal workers. They also had a virtual monopoly on the silk and dyeing industries.

The Sicilian Jewish community, an integral and vital part of this unique cultural microcosm of their island, was the most important in the Mediterranean. Though the darker times for the Sicilian Jewry began in the 14th century with the establishment of the Aragonese (Spanish) rule, compared to the Jews of other European countries, or even other regions of Italy, the Sicilian Jews experienced little hostility from either Muslims or Christians until the Edict of 1492.

The Triumph of Death at the Palazzo Abatellis Gallery

This 15th-century Gothic-Catalan palazzo that is currently an art museum contains a curious, little-noticed, and rarely-discussed example of that uniquely Sicilian pre-expulsion attitude toward the Jews. Bianca suggested we go to the Palazzo Abatellis to take a close look at the late gothic-style fresco, called "The Triumph of Death."

This work of an unknown artist is dated around the 1440s. The fresco shows Death on a skinny white horse galloping through a beautiful garden, which symbolizes life itself. The grotesque grimacing horse is placed in the center of the composition. Its rider, Death, is shooting deadly arrows at people in the garden. The fresco's characters represent all social classes, and on the bottom we see the corpses of those already killed: emperors, popes, and bishops. On the right, Death seems to target the richly dressed nobles, while on the left, are the pious and the poor that are spared. Only two characters in this group are looking directly at the viewer. Perhaps these were the patron or sponsor and the artist himself. The fresco's overall composition and the message were common for the 14th and the 15th centuries. Highly unusual was the depiction of a Jew in the left group of the pious. Just fifty years before the forced expulsion of the Jews from the island, an unknown artist depicted the Jews as deserving to be spared by Death.

The Expulsion

In 1492, striving to maintain Catholic orthodoxy and "purify" their kingdom, the Spanish monarchs Ferdinand and Isabella ordered the forced expulsion or conversion of all Jews in their lands on pain of death. Though the exact estimates are not available, historians suggest that there were probably 52 Jewish communities spread out across Sicily, numbering somewhere between 35,000 to 40,000 people, though some sources estimate the number to be closer to 100,000. Rabbi Barbara believes that about 40 percent of the Sicilian and Calabrian population at the time of the Edict could have been Jews. The infamous Edict of Expulsion brought an end to the flourishing Jewish culture in Sicily and to the highly important role the Jews played in the regional economy. Palermo archives contain period letters from the local governments, who, fearful of the collapse of banking and commerce, pleaded with the Monarchs to change their minds. In Palermo, by some accounts, Jews constituted over 10 percent of the population and their wealth influenced the four-month extension of the expulsion final date, most probably in order to prolong the looting.

Seeking Palermian Jewish voices after 500 years of silence

On the way to the Jewish Quarter

My friend Bianca was determined to help us find traces of the long-gone Jewish life in her city, "even if we have to travel through layers of concrete and centuries of ignorance," she said. In reality, to get to the narrow medieval streets of the former Jewish district, we had to travel through the splendor of the Palermian Renaissance and Baroque. We marveled at Piazza Pretoria with its magnificent 16th-century fountain originally built for a Tuscan villa. The fountain's seductive nudes played in the water as we hurried by. We admired the exquisite Baroque of the Quattro Canti, where the four corners (quattro canti) are formed by two major avenues, Via Maqueda and Corso Vittorio Emanuele. The piazza is actually octagonal, formed by four buildings with nearly identical facades decorated with fountains and gorgeous female statues representing the four seasons. Frivolity and naked beauty of the 15th and 16th centuries clashes with the severity of 12th-century Arab-Norman structures: the nearby churches of La Martorana and San Cataldo. After visiting the churches, we found ourselves right in the middle of Palermo's Judaic legacy, *La Giudecca.*

La Giudecca

Unlike the European ghettos that were locked in from the outside, Sicilian Jews lived in La Giudecca, an open city district or a quarter that offered free passage and that was freely chosen by the Jews to be near their fellow co-religionists. We walked through narrow ancient streets that used to follow the curve of the river Kemonia, now Via Andrea Giardinaccio. The oldest houses in La Giudecca had a peculiar fixture specific to Palermo called the *gheniza* or a groove in the front door where the house owner kept a small roll with a passage from the Torah. The Jewish district most likely extended as far west as Salita dell Ospedale in the L'Albergheria quarter, a probable location of an ancient Jewish hospital. In 2003, Professor Niccolo Bucaria announced his controversial discovery of a 10th-century Miqweh, a ritual Jewish bath, under the 15th-century Palazzo Marchesi. The Jesuits built their Church of Santa Maria del Gesu or Casa Professa on the site of the Palazzo. This discovery provoked numerous arguments on whether the structure of what was long believed to be a water reservoir pointed to the location of a second synagogue. Perhaps due to the controversy, the Miqweh of Palermo is not as famous or as touristy as the Miqweh of Siracusa.

Among the prominent sons of La Giudecca in Palermo were the celebrated court physician Master Busach, famous translator from Arabic Moses of Palermo, distinguished scholar David Ahitub, and renowned astronomer Isaac Al'dahav. I repeat their names aloud a few times over to evoke these great ghosts of the past. In 1393, said Bianca, King Martin I issued a decree by which Jews of Palermo, inhabitants of this neighborhood, were appointed as a court of appeals in all legal disputes among Jews in all of Sicily. The importance given by the local government to the Jews of Palermo's La Giudecca is illustrated by a documented fact: in 1491, just a year before the Edict, the intervention of the Palermian Jews prevented the sale of Jewish refugees from Provence as slaves.

Recently, the City of Palermo installed brown-and-white street signs which, in Palermian multicultural style, show the street names in three languages: Italian, Hebrew, and Arabic. Many streets were named after the inhabitants' professions, such as Via Calderai for boilermakers or Via Lamponelli for lantern-makers. One street sign reads: Vicolo Meschita, the mosque.

The Meschita

The Great Synagogue, admired by numerous travelers from all corners of the earth, was the center of the Jewish quarter. "Palermo's Synagogue is without equal the world over," wrote one Ovadyah Yare of Bertinoro in 1487. Architectural historians think that the synagogue structure most probably resembled other Norman-Arab buildings of worship of the time: square in shape, Romanesque in style, and with graceful arches and a cupola. In the 17th century, the church and the monastery of St. Nicolo Tolentino were built on the site of the Great Synagogue of Palermo. In the late 19th century, part of the synagogue's and the monastery's ruins were rebuilt as the City Archives. The street nearby is called Via Meschita or the mosque. Was it ignorance that prompted Sicilian Christians to name the synagogue street "the Mosque?" Or was it a historic memory? The physical place occupied by the entire La Giudecca since the 10th century used to be the Arab quarter. During the Norman period and centuries after, the Jewish neighborhood shared a border with a Greek quarter and an Arab souk called *Bah'lara*, which survives today as the Ballaro street market.

We visited La Giudecca on Wednesday afternoon, when most Palermo markets were closed but Ballaro was open. We went there and enjoyed its smells, colors, and noise. The market's vibrant life served as another poignant reminder of the silenced voices and extinguished lives of the flourishing Jewish community whose ghosts we left behind.

From the market, we headed to another medieval neighborhood, La Kalsa, from the Arabic *Al-Khalisa*, or "the purest." The formal name of this district is Mandamento Tribunali, the "district of courts." The name is derived from the menacing presence of the infamous Inquisition Courts in Palazzo Steri.

Palazzo Steri: graffiti, tears, and auto-da-fe

The building

The imposing 14th-century building was originally constructed as the private residence of the powerful Sicilian lord Manfredi III Chiaramonte. The palatial fortress style of the structure and its curious mixture of Romanesque and the Gothic elements became known across the Mediterranean as the Chiaramonte Gothic. In the beginning of the 16th century, this palace became the residence of the Aragonese-Spanish viceroys of Sicily. Later, it housed the Royal Customs. But the palace owns its infamous place in history between the years 1600 and 1782, when it served as the tribunal of the Holy Inquisition. The façade shows the grooves left by iron cages used to display the severed heads of the nobles who had rebelled against the Holy Roman Emperor Charles V.

The prisoners

Today, the palace is a museum dedicated to those who suffered within the Steri walls, including the converted or *neofiti* Jews accused of secretly practicing their old faith. According to "Tracing the Tribe: The Jewish Genealogy Blog" and other sources, neofiti Jews were the focus of the 1516 Palermo riot. A generation after the Expulsion, the Palermian new Christians were still identified as Jews, and persecuted as such, denounced to the Inquisition, and often executed.

We entered the former Inquisition prison and followed Bianca from one claustrophobic cell to another. What we found was an astonishing art gallery: 16th through 18th-century graffiti covering the walls almost from top to bottom. This gallery represents a rare glimpse into the prisoners' torments, inner struggles with their own demons, and attempts to convince the inquisitors of their innocence. While prisoners' wall drawings are not uncommon, what is unique for the Steri prison is that most of the graffiti are not anonymous but signed, dated, and accompanied by often highly literate descriptions. The artistic skills are very impressive and so is the inmates' erudition.

The 16 cells open to the public occupy two floors of the museum. One cell is identified as the place in which a monk, the legendary Diego La Matina, snapped during his torture and killed his inquisitor with his chains. This episode was immortalized by a famous Sicilian writer Leonardo Sciascia in his novella Morte dell'Inquisitore. In another cell, we stayed for a long time studying a detailed drawing depicting 16 figures with Jewish names such as Abraham, Moses, his brother Aaron, Adam and Eve, and others that identify them as the twelve tribes of Israel. They are coming out of the mouth of a giant menacing-looking fish (Leviathan?) with a big cross on its head (the Church?) to a possible salvation impersonated by a strange angel with a devil's tail wearing a crown of thorns on his head. Was that an unfortunate neofiti trying to convince his executors of his supposedly true Christian faith? But it was in a cell empty of graffiti where we could not hold back our tears. "In December 2013," said Bianca, "in this cell, we had a Hanukah candle-lighting ceremony accompanied by singing of Hebrew liturgy."

No matter what was done to us, we thought, it appears that we, the Jews, are indeed indestructible, a truly eternal people. Hundreds of years after the forced expulsion and conversions, tortures and executions, our spirit is alive and our voices are heard.

The auto-da-fe in Palermo

Sentencing the accused or auto-da-fe was staged as a combination of grand public entertainment and a solemn holy day with all shops and offices closed throughout the city. This ceremony took place either on the Cathedral Square or in front of the Palazzo Steri. The entire spectacle was designed to impress and teach the masses. The condemned were burned at the stake on the square near the Steri, now a park called Villa Garibaldi. We left the museum and proceeded to this peaceful green park to contemplate the Sicilian story of anti-Semitism and persecution. June 6th, 2011, explained Bianca, marked the 500-year anniversary of the first mass execution by the Inquisition of "Judaizing" heretics on that very square.

Nadia Zeldes's study "Auto da Fe in Palermo 1511" published in *Revue de L'Histoire des Religions* in 2002 is one of the best available English scholarly articles focusing on the early executions of Palermo's B'nei Anousim. Since all Inquisition records were destroyed after the institution itself was abolished in Sicily in 1782, Zeldes's research relies on the descriptions of eyewitnesses and on the Holy Office's accounting books.

Zeldes writes that in Palermo two platforms were built right below the windows of the Steri palace. One was for the inquisitors and people of the church and another for the accused who were usually seated at different heights according to their crimes, among which "Judaizing" was considered the highest.

"Judaizing" heretics were the neofiti suspected of practicing their old faith. Sicily was the only place outside of Spain and Portugal where, in the late 15th century, a large part of the population had to quickly convert to Christianity and therefore become a subject of suspicion, persecution, and Inquisition. Estimates of how many Sicilian Jews chose to leave the island and how many converted to Christianity vary. The number was considered threatening enough, however, to justify decades of persecution of the converts and their descendants. Little is known about the real extent and practices of the crypto-Jews in Palermo outside of what the Inquisition called the "Judaizing." These "crimes" included adherence to Jewish religious customs, like circumcising their male children; observing Sabbath on Saturday rather than Sunday; and refusing to eat pork. One young woman was thrown in prison and tortured because neighbors denounced her for changing her undergarments on Friday.

Zeldes describes how the Inquisition was established in Palermo to explain at what point a diverse and multicultural society of that great city turned into a place where neighbors were enthusiastically denouncing each other. Though the Spanish Inquisition existed in Sicily since 1487, the Holy Office was known to "find nothing against Sicilians." In 1510, a new enthusiastic and energetic Inquisitor was appointed who promised informers a fifth of the property of every "heretic" that they helped to uncover. This simple incentive marked the end of the tolerant microcosm of Palermo and produced a sudden spike of arrests and executions.

Jewish cultural renaissance of the 21st century

In her article "The Italian Anousim that Nobody Knows" (2009) Rabbi Barbara Aiello, a founder of the Italian Jewish Cultural Center of Calabria, quotes her colleague Professor Vincenzo Villella, who is convinced that many researchers of Jewish history often make a "grave error." They assume that elimination of institutional Judaism meant the end of Judaism itself. Burning synagogues and the neofiti forced Italian Jews to take their traditions into the cellars and secret rooms of their homes. The memories and stories were kept alive, even when descendants forgot their exact meaning. And, as Rabbi Barbara writes, the number of those with a "call of blood," who think they have Jewish ancestry and want to learn more about it, or even embrace their newly-discovered heritage, is on the rise throughout southern Italy.

In Sicily, Bianca told me her acquaintance, a French Jew, Evelyn Aouate, founded the ISSE (Sicilian Institute for Hebrew Studies) headquartered at the University of Palermo. In September 2014, during European Jewish Culture Week, the ISSE organized numerous Jewish heritage-centered activities, including a Klezmorim concert that took place at the City Archives located on the holy ground of the destroyed Great Synagogue. Outside of the official

Jewish Culture Week, many events highlighting the Jewish history of Palermo take place throughout the year. One of the most emotional experiences Bianca told us about was a menorah lighting ceremony inside the Steri prison cells during Hanukkah.

Bianca showed us another manifestation of the new Jewish history awareness in Palermo: the Garden of the Righteous. Surrounded by centuries-old walls, an ancient courtyard of the now non-existing palace was reborn in 2008 as a memorial garden dedicated to those around the world who saved their Jewish neighbors during the Holocaust. The guest of honor during the dedication ceremony was the Mayor of Tel-Aviv. The initiator of the Gardens movement was writer Gabriel Nissim, who wrote a book about the Anousim *Ebrei Invisibli* translated as the "invisible Jews." When Nissim organized The Gardens of the Righteous Worldwide Committee, the Municipality of Palermo decided to create this kind of garden in their own city.

Classes on Hebrew, Jewish culture, and art are held all over Palermo. On Bianca's initiative, a class called "Interpretation of Genesis from the Jewish Perspective" was offered in 2015 to an enthusiastic audience of tour guides.

In 2011, Rabbi Barbara Aiello officiated a Bar Mitzvah ceremony of Salvo Asher Parrucca, the first Bar Mitzvah in Palermo in 500 years. Mr. Parrucca, the first anousim in Palermo, is studying for his rabbinate. We were not able to talk with Mr. Parrucca during our time in Palermo: it was right before the High Holidays and Mr. Parrucca was out of town. To meet the first Sicilian-born and Sicilian-based Rabbi we traveled to Siracusa.

*About the Contributor

Bianca Del Bello, both a Sicilian and Northern Italian, was born in Belgium. As a child, she lived in various European countries, returning to Palermo, Sicily with her parents when she was 18. Bianca studied European languages at the University of Palermo and became a tour guide. A historian and a polyglot, Bianca enjoys Sicily, "the island of one thousand identities," and shares her passionate love and deep knowledge of the island with her tourists. Bianca's contribution to this article in terms of fact checking and Jewish Renaissance events in Palermo is invaluable.

Selected Sources

Keahey, J. Seeking Sicily: A Cultural Journey through Myth and Reality in the Heart of the Mediterranean. Thomad Dunne Books, 2011.

Lampedusa, Di, G. The Leopard. Reprint Edition. Random House, 2013.

Robb, P. Midnight in Sicily. Picador, 2007.

Simonsohn, S. The Jews in Sicily, 383-1300. Brill Academic Publishing, 1997.

Zeldes, N. The Former Jews of This Kingdom: Sicilian Converts After the Expulsion 1492-1516. Brill Academic Publishing, 2003.

Zeldes, N. "Auto da Fe in Palermo 1511." Revue de L'Histoire des Religions, 2002.

Palermo Cathedral's bell tower with Moorish ornaments on Arabic-style double windows.

The Palermo Cathedral demonstrates Norman Gothic arches and Arabic decorations.

"The Triumph of Death" fresco at the Palazzo Abatellis gallery in Palermo.

"The Triumph of Death" fresco depicts a Jewish figure among the pious spared by Death.

In Palermian multicultural style, the streets' names are shown in three languages: Italian, Hebrew, and Arabic.

In Palermo, the Vicolo Meschita, the street where synagogue used to stand, is named after a mosque.

The churches of La Martorana (left) and San Cataldo (right). The Great Synagogue of Palermo most probably resembled the Norman-Arabic style houses of worship, like these churches.

The Church of San Cataldo. The Jewish Star is clearly visible in the upper left window. Courtesy of Bianca Del Bello.

151

La Giudecca. In Palermo, unlike other European Jewish ghettoes, the Jews lived in an open city district that offered free passage.

St. Nicolo church was built in the 17th century on the site of the Great Synagogue of Palermo.

The City of Palermo Archives building was erected in the 19th century on part of the Great Synagogue's site.

The Ballaro market in Palermo. La Giudecca was bordered by an Arab souk "Bah'lara," which survives today as the Ballaro market.

Exquisite Palermo Baroque: Piazza Pretoria with its magnificent 16th-century fountain. Beautiful nudes are playing in the water.

A masterpiece of Palermo Baroque: Piazza Quattro Canti (four corners). The corners are formed by two major avenues.

Phoenician wall in Palermo. Phoenicians, great sea traders from the Persian Gulf, were the first group to colonize Sicily.

The Roman wall in Palermo.

The 14th-century Palazzo Steri, now the Palermo Museum of the Inquisition.

Entrance to the Palazzo Steri. Among the prisoners were the converted Jews accused of secretly practicing their old faith.

A drawing in the Palazzo Steri depicting figures with Jewish names who are coming out of the mouth of a giant fish with a cross on its head.

The Vespers Square in Palermo with the Palazzo Gangi. This palace was chosen by movie director Luciano Visconti as the setting for the ballroom scene in his masterpiece *The Leopard*.

Villa Garibaldi, a peaceful green park now, was where the condemned were often burned at the stake. Courtesy of Bianca Del Bello.

The Garden of the Righteous in Palermo is dedicated to those who saved their Jewish neighbors during the Holocaust.

The Sicilian Jewish History Conference took place inside the City Archives in 2014. Courtesy of Giuliana Torre and the Sicilian Institute for Hebrew Studies.

A Professor from the University of Palermo reads the Edict of Expulsion during the Sicilian Jewish History Conference. Courtesy of Giuliana Torre and the Sicilian Institute for Hebrew Studies.

Klezmorim concert at the Palermo City Archives. The clarinetist is
Giovanni Mattaliano. Jewish Culture Week, September 2014.
Courtesy of Giuliana Torre and the Sicilian Institute for Hebrew
Studies.

Siracusa is the true personification of Sicily: the city combines traces of Greek and Roman civilizations with ancient Jewish culture and baroque masterpieces.

The City Where Jewish History Comes to Life

Siracusa the Great

Siracusa is truly a summation of Sicilian splendor, and if there is one city in Sicily that personifies this magnificent island it is Siracusa. This 3,000-year-old city-in-the-making combines Greek and Roman civilizations with ancient Jewish culture and Baroque masterpieces. Founded in 734 BC by Greeks from Corinth, Siracusa grew quickly to become a city larger than Corinth and Athens, turning into the capital of Magna Crecia. It became an intellectual magnet that attracted the best brain power of the ancient world, from Aeschylus and Pindar of theater and poetry, to Archimedes, the genius of mathematics and physics. The Romans invaded Siracusa in 211 BC, killing Archimedes and the city's splendor along with him. Even though Siracusa remained the capital of Sicily under the Romans, its glory days were over. When it was taken over by the Saracen Arabs, Siracusa was reduced to a provincial fortified town. Ironically, a 17th-century earthquake served as a catalyst for the city's renewal, and beautiful baroque buildings and squares came into being.

Today, visitors come to Siracusa enticed by its two main attractions: the Ortygia island with its magnificent Duomo Square and a tangled maze of historic alleyways, and the world-renowned Greek and Roman Archeological Park of Neapolis. For Jewish history pilgrims, Siracusa has one of the most charming Jewish quarters in Italy with its recently discovered Miqwe (Jewish ritual bath), the oldest in Europe.

It is also the only city on the island where one can visit the first synagogue and the first Rabbi in modern Sicily since the Edict of Expulsion of 1492.

Rav Di Mauro of Siracusa: a present-day Biblical Moses

We drove for about 30 minutes from the medieval Ortygia into the contemporary city of Siracusa to find Via Italia near the Tribunale Nuovo. The number 88 building had a large sign on its iron gate: "Sinagoga di Siracusa" adorned with a menorah made up of Hebrew words that tell the story of this congregation. We rang the bell and stepped into a small courtyard. The sign on the building read: "Comunita Ebraica di Siracusa. Affiliata alla Federazione Comunita Ebraiche dei Mediterrano." The synagogue occupies the ground floor of an apartment building. Rav Di Mauro welcomed us inside. He had a warm smile that immediately put us at ease. With his white long beard and deep long gaze, the Rabbi reminded me of the Biblical saints from mosaics in Capella Palatina and Monreale cathedral. After a tour of the delightful one-room synagogue, we sat down with the Rabbi to hear his story.

A native of Siracusa, our new friend Stefano Di Mauro, MD (Cardiology), PhD (Psychology and Nutrition), was educated in both Italy and the United States. For many decades he had his successful medical practice in North Miami Beach, Florida. While still a medical student in Sicily, Di Mauro found out that his classmate was secretly seeking to convert to Judaism. Why? Because, the young man explained, he always knew that he was Jewish. "You see," the Rabbi told us, "for the Sicilian Anousim, this gut feeling, this inescapable 'I-always-knew' voice was the main driver. Historical facts did not matter. Evidence did not matter." The Rabbi spoke from his own experience of searching for his inner spiritual self for as long as he remembered. The friend's disclosure was followed by Stefano's mother's death-bed confession of the family's Jewish origins concealed for over 500 years. The dying woman told her son how she and other families bound together by the undisclosed knowledge were trying to live in the same neighborhood, making sure their children played and studied together, an undying hope for sustaining the secret blood line. During the many years that followed, Doctor Di Mauro continued to practice medicine while studying Judaism at the same time. He eventually formally converted to Orthodox Judaism and completed his rabbinical studies and ordination in both Jerusalem and Miami.

The Rabbi proudly showed us his framed ordination license. "As a Rabbi and a leader of the congregation, I am not recognized by Rome," he revealed to us. "Rome always viewed with suspicion whatever was happening here on the island. We were a conquered colony for over 3,000 years. Nothing changed much." What did change a great deal, however, was Jewish life in Siracusa.

In 2007, the 68 year-old Dr. Di Mauro left his successful practice in Florida and with his young American wife and two little children moved to his hometown, Siracusa. Here on the island, in 2008 he established the first Jewish congregation in over 500 years. The Siracusa city administration did not permit the Rabbi to either buy or rent the property for his synagogue on the touristy Ortygia, so Di Mauro returned to his old neighborhood in the outskirts of the city. "It is symbolic," said the Rabbi, never the one to be stopped by any obstacles. "This is the area where the Jewish traders settled when they arrived with the Greeks in Hellenistic times, long before the medieval La Giudecca was established on the island of Ortygia." Led by this 21st-century Moses-like man, the inspired congregation now counts about 40 people. Holidays might bring international visitors. Purim is becoming especially popular with guests arriving from as far as Australia.

The Rabbi who brought to life the long-suppressed Jewish story of Siracusa had also revived a long-forgotten tradition of the island, that of *Purim Katan*. Some sources (i.e., "Sicily's Ancient Jewish Presence," by Giovanni Frazzetto, *Haaretz*, Jan. 2013) state that this unique ritual had long been misattributed to the Spanish city of Saragossa, but historians recently recognized that it actually originated in Siracusa. The story tells of a supposedly historic event when during the reign of the Aragonese King Martin I, the Jews of Siracusa were spared a terrible punishment. The Rabbi told us that the Siracusa's Megillah narrated how for many years, each time the King visited the Giudecca he was greeted by a procession of elders representing the 12 synagogues in town who presented him the Torah as a sign of their submission. Eventually the Jews decided that the Torah should not be made to bow to the King, and only the empty wooden cases would be shown to him. The years went by, and the King never knew that he was shown only empty Torah cases. One year, a converso who sought the King's favor disclosed this secret to the King who became enraged and vowed to punish all the city's Jews. It was not the Esther of the traditional Purim story, but the Prophet Elijah himself who saved his people in Siracusa. He revealed the plot in a dream to a guardian of one of the synagogues. This time, the real Torah scrolls were shown to the King and the Jews were saved. And so it happened, that in January 2013, for the first time in more than 500 years, Siracusans listened to their Rabbi read their own Megillah in their new synagogue.

Ebrei di Ritorno (Returning Jews)

"You have to keep in mind," said the Rabbi, "this island has had a vibrant Jewish life for over two thousand years. Siracusa was thirty percent Jewish before the Edict. Entire villages on the island sometimes were descendants of Jews that preserved their Jewishness in secret. I see my mission as to help these people to recapture the awareness of their roots." The Rabbi, who is now 75 years old, is not slowing down. In 2012, he helped to organize a two-day conference in Siracusa supported by the Union of Italian Communities, the umbrella association for the Italian Jewish organizations, and by the Shavei Israel, an Israel-based foundation that reaches out to Jewish descendants around the world. Three of his students were planning to leave Siracusa in 2015 to continue their rabbinical studies, become ordained, and hopefully return to their home city. Inspired by Siracusa's own son, the Jews of Siracusa, forgotten for too long, are coming back home. Centuries after the Inquisition sought to burn Judaism at the stake, the new Jewish community came to live again in one of the greatest cities of the Mediterranean and brought along the secret stories of identity and traditions that were carried from generation to generation.

Jewish Ortygia in Siracusa

Leaving the synagogue, we traveled to Ortygia, a beautifully preserved ancient island where a Greek urban framework still remains for almost three millennia. The streets have a "comb teeth" orientation as they emanate from the Greeks' Sacred Way, now Via Dione, running through the center of the island. The eastern part of Ortygia is called La Giudecca with streets named after those who lived and prospered there for many centuries: Via Giudecca, Vicolo

Giudecca I, II, III, and IV. While thinking of the Rabbi's stories evoking the ghosts of the Jewish past, we walked along these charming narrow vicoli (alleys) crowned with wrought-iron miniature balconies with flower pots.

Rav Di Mauro explained that the Jews settled on the east side of Ortygia because they wanted to symbolically face Jerusalem. Here stood homes of the most populous Jewish community on the island after that of Palermo, and arguably the most ancient. All buildings in Giudecca including shops, schools, bakeries, and private homes were constructed, according to the ancient Middle Eastern custom, around the courtyard, in the center of which was a palm and an olive or a citrus tree, which some said survived till today. The prosperity of the Siracusa community was well documented by the Roman tax collectors who kept records of noted wealthy Jewish bankers and merchants. In the first century AD, the community was important enough for St. Paul to arrive there in 59 AD and preach Christianity to the Jews of Ortygia. The twelve synagogues of Siracusa located in Giudecca undoubtedly heard many philosophical debates of local and visiting scholars over the centuries. The last well-known Jewish scholar from Sicily was Siracusa's son Joseph Saragosi, a Kabbalist and Talmudist, and the founder of the mystic school in Safed.

The Synagogue

While traces of most of the twelve synagogues are lost to history, one location is now well-known. The Church of San Giovanni Battista (John the Baptist) was most probably built on the ruins of the main synagogue, where, as researchers maintain, St. Paul preached to the Siracusans. Archeologists found out that the synagogue, just like other buildings in the Giudecca, was constructed around a large enclosed courtyard, which, after the Jews were exiled and the synagogue ruined, was broken up to create the square Piazza del Precursore. The synagogue originally had a different orientation than the church into which it was converted. The adaption was hasty and the beautiful Gothic-style entrance now looks off-center. The church was almost destroyed during the earthquake of the 17th century and now has no roof. This site is often used for summer concerts.

To the immediate right of the church's entrance stands the house where Mario Minniti lived. A native of Siracusa, Mario was a painter, a friend, a follower, and perhaps, a lover of the great Caravaggio, whom he met while living in Rome. Mario was probably instrumental in helping a fugitive Caravaggio who was accused of a murder to secure the Santa Lucia Church's commission in Siracusa. Today, "The Burial of Santa Lucia," a masterpiece of this eccentric Italian genius is exhibited near the church's altar. Art lovers and Caravaggio fans may recognize Mario Minniti's face from the artist's well-known paintings: The Lute Player in the Hermitage, Russia; Bacchus in the Uffizi Gallery, Florence; and Fortune Teller in the Capitoline Museums of Rome. In addition to Mario's role in the history of Italian Baroque painting, Caravaggio's friend unknowingly played an important part in the Jewish history of Siracusa. He "helped" the archeologists to find out about the former location of the entrance to the synagogue: Mario repeatedly complained to city authorities and finally obtained permission to demolish the arch of the neighboring church's main door which hung over the alley that runs along his home.

The Miqwe

Leaving Mario's house and St. John's Church, we headed to Via Alagona, one of the most picturesque medieval streets in Giudecca. There, in the Alla Giudecca Hotel, we were scheduled to visit a rare site, a treat for any Jewish history pilgrim: an ancient Jewish ritual bath or Miqwe (mikveh, mikvah) that is located 18 meters (59 feet) beneath street level. The Miqwe can be seen only on the guided tour.

Built in the 6th century AD during the Byzantine period in Sicily, this oldest known Miqwe in Europe was completely hidden in the 15th century, blocked and camouflaged by the Jews of Siracusa, when they were forced into exile. In 1987, architects working on the conversion of an old building into a hotel noticed a strange arrangement of courtyard stones. They discovered that the stones covered the "ceiling" of an underground chamber. The hotel guide told us that several truckloads of rubbish had to be removed to uncover an ancient limestone staircase leading to a large rectangular room, entirely cut through stone and supported by four pillars. This principal room contains three pools filled with fresh water. Two additional pools are situated in smaller adjacent rooms. Ventilation and light are provided by an opening in the ceiling, now located next to the current access to the stairs. Additional light probably came from many oil lamps discovered by archeologists and displayed in the hotel's lobby in glass cases. Since Miqwe water has to be "live" or flowing without any human intervention, the archeologists had to make sure they bore deeply into subsoil to reach the ancient water source.

In traditional Judaism, the Miqwe is given the same importance as the synagogue. Jaqueline Alio, a renowned Sicilian historian, commented that in medieval Italy, a new Jewish community would first build their Miqwe, and then collect the funds for a synagogue or a Torah scroll. Ritual bathing or tevilah (full-body immersion) for both women and men is sacred for Judaism and symbolizes purification. Researchers believe that tevilah became an inspiration for baptism in Christianity or for ghusl in Islam, as a shared spiritual renewal ritual for all three Abrahamic religions.

In the last fifty years, other early medieval Miqwe were discovered in Europe, and all of them became museum pieces as in London (2001) or national historic sites as in Cologne (1956). What makes the Siracusa Miqwe, the oldest of all known, so different, is that since Rabbi Di Mauro started the rebirth of Jewish life in his native city, the Miqwe has been used continuously. Rav Di Mauro performed 10 conversions so far and even one wedding at the Miqwe. As the Rabbi said, this fifteen-hundred-year-old Miqwe is a true living legacy and testimony to the undying spirit and light of Judaism.

Selected Sources

Dummet, J. Syracuse, City of Legends: A Glory of Sicily. I. B. Tauris Books, 2015.

Freund, M. "Jewish Life in Sicily Reborn," Shavei Israel, September 2011.

The magnificent Duomo Square on the ancient Ortygia island.

The world-renowned Greek amphitheater in the Archeological Park of Neapolis, Siracusa.

Only in Siracusa one can see the Roman amphitheater (pictured) side by side with the Greek theater (previous photo).

Entrance to the Synagogue of Siracusa, the first synagogue in Sicily since 1492.

Sign on the Synagogue of Siracusa.

The Synagogue's interior. The synagogue occupies the ground floor of an apartment building.

Rav Di Mauro, the first Rabbi in Sicily after 500 years since the Edict of Expulsion.

The author with Rabbi Di Mauro.

The Siracusa Torah scrolls.

Rabbi Di Mauro proudly demonstrates his ordination certificates from Jerusalem and Miami, Florida.

Purim celebration in the Synagogue of Siracusa. Courtesy of Rav
Di Mauro.

Entering the ancient Jewish Quarter, La Giudecca of Ortygia,
Siracusa.

In the Jewish neighborhood of Siracusa: a tangled maze of historic alleyways laid out by ancient Greeks.

The church of San Giovanni Battista was most probably built on the ruins of the main Siracusa synagogue.

Entrance to the Miqwe of Siracusa built in the 6th century AD, the oldest known Miqwe in Europe.

The Miqwe. Since Rabbi Di Mauro started the rebirth of Jewish life in Siracusa, the Miqwe has been used continuously. Courtesy of Bianca Del Bello.

Medieval streets of Taormina.

"A Little Patch of Paradise"

Following the steps of Tennessee Williams

Inspired by Siracusa, we continued our personal search for Jewish history in other Sicilian cities. Taormina, our next destination, was a double magnet: one of the medieval centers of Jewish culture, this city was also the place where my favorite playwright Tennessee Williams, the subject of both my thesis and my first book, spent many happy months with his beloved partner, poet Henry Faulkner. Williams and Faulkner stayed in Taormina's "Casa Cuseni." I always knew without a doubt, that when we were in Sicily, in addition to my Jewish history research, we would also follow the steps of Tennessee!

We arrived in Taormina late in the afternoon. In the fall at that time of the day, Taormina is lit by magical shades of a golden-blue light coming from above and below, from the sky and the sea, which turns the city into *la bella Trinacria*, Dante's name for Sicily. One of the most beautiful cities of Sicily, Taormina was called by Goethe "a little patch of paradise." Many first-time visitors today may find it hard to believe the great German poet after seeing streets and restaurants of the "paradise" literally occupied by crowds of tourists, while its cathedrals and palaces are taken over by unending wedding ceremonies. But crowds and people-jammed streets are nothing new to Taormina. For the last one hundred years or so, Taormina has been a flashy resort for Europe's rich and famous. One of the city's popular cocktails is called "Liz" after Elizabeth Taylor, who reportedly invented the recipe.

Indeed, on the surface, the city is unashamedly touristy and distinctly un-Sicilian. But if you are willing to look beyond its glitzy surface, you will be richly rewarded. Taormina's Teatro Greco, arguably the most beautiful of the surviving ancient Greek theaters, is carved out of the slope of a mountain with the sea, sky, and volcano Etna serving as its natural backdrops. Sitting on one of the marble benches inside the theater and slowly absorbing the breathtaking view around you is a deeply spiritual experience. The city's supernatural beauty, its medieval streets, Roman mosaic floors, and Norman-Arabic churches create an indescribable atmosphere, and the city turns into a magic world after dark.

In the 19th century, this most beautiful of Sicilian cities became a refuge for artists, like Oscar Wilde, who were exiled from their home countries. Taormina turned into an intellectual oasis for those whose views or lifestyles were not considered moral or conventional, like D. H. Lawrence, Tennessee Williams, Henry Faulkner, and Truman Capote. They often congregated in Casa Cuseni hotel, getting together over drinks on its rooftop that overlooked that magic town with the volcano Etna in the background. We chose this remarkable house as our home away from home in Taormina.

At Casa Cuseni we were met by the B&B's smiling owner, Francesco Spadaro, an MD, collector and art lover. We followed him up the stairs through a terraced garden. For us, Casa Cuseni embodied the best that Taormina had to offer. Just like Taormina is not your typical Sicilian town, Casa Cuseni is not the B&B one may expect. This house is a destination by itself, a living museum of arts and letters, "a place where Art has found its Home," as Francesco Spadaro calls it.

This villa was designed and built by the leading member of the British Royal Academy of Arts, painter Robert Hawthorn Kitson, in 1905. For Kitson, Casa Cuseni became a refuge, a cultural universe away from the world of Victorian morals and his Yorkshire family with their judgmental attitudes toward his lifestyle. Since Kitson was an Art Nouveau or rather, Arts & Crafts artist in love with Italy and Sicily, the house and gardens he designed present a harmonious mixture of the continental Art Nouveau and Sicilian Liberty styles. Robert Kitson's teacher and friend Frank Brangwyn designed the paneling and furniture, and created a mural in the dining room. This beautiful, elegant, and refined mural invokes a poignant feeling of being singled out and ostracized. Brangwyn figures symbolize homosexual love, threatened and persecuted by society.

When Robert Kitson died in 1948, his niece, Daphne Phelps, came all the way from Great Britain to Sicily to sell the house. But she fell in love with the place, the country, and the people. She decided to stay and rent out several rooms to paying guests. Daphne went on to write A House in Sicily, one of the best books about this island.

This house, as shown by its wonderful manager Salvatore, had come alive for us and turned into one of the main characters of Sicily. In addition to the beautiful furnishings and mural, the house's treasures are displayed everywhere. Staying in Casa Cuseni, we found ourselves inside a living and breathing museum surrounded by Picasso, Faulkner, and Kitson, plus the countless treasures from Kitson's personal collection, such as Sumerian, Greek, early medieval, and Renaissance priceless pieces. I was particularly impressed and deeply touched by Salvatore spending over an hour of his time to share the collection of Tennessee Williams's writings and private letters.

Though inseparable from Taormina, Casa Cuseni is a world treasure, a must destination for any art and literature lover.

However, it was time for us to return to our Jewish story. Following the footsteps of those who were forced into the oblivion of history over five hundred years ago proved a much more challenging task than trying to resurrect the times of Tennessee Williams or Oscar Wilde.

Tracing Jewish history with the local police

Knowing that Taormina used to have a large and prosperous Jewish community dating back to the Hellenistic Greeks, we were looking for any traces of that past. I remembered coming across a photo of a Taormina street sign saying "Del Ghetto." That seemed strange, since Sicilian Jews did not usually live in ghettos, though with the Aragonese (Spanish) rule in the late 1300s, Jews experienced discrimination in Sicily, and in some places were mandated to live in ghettos. Perhaps Taormina was one of those cities.

Since no one we questioned at bookshops, a municipal building, or tourist information knew where to find the street named "Del Ghetto," we asked the local police.

Two police officers, a man and a woman, stopped their patrol car in the middle of the Duomo square and with great enthusiasm spent almost an hour on my "find the Jews" project. The policewoman called somebody on her cell phone, turned on her radio, and holding my crumbled copy of the street sign photo, gesticulated energetically while loudly explaining something in rapid Sicilian to at least a couple of people she talked to simultaneously. The policeman climbed out of the car and took me around the square pointing at signs like "Salita Ibrahim," and "Via Ebrei," or Jewish stars on the municipal building that was erected on the site of the main synagogue. I understood that when we passed through the medieval clock tower gate, we entered the Jewish Quarter where a few of the street signs and an occasional Jewish star were the only remaining vestiges of the Taormina Jewish people, now lost to history and memory. To their sincere disappointment, our new friends from the local police could not find the "Del Ghetto" sign. Perhaps, the officers tried to explain to me in their broken English, "they," the policeman pointed to the municipal building, decided to take the sign off.

Selected Sources

Phelps, D. A House in Sicily. Da Capo Press, 2000.

Von Gloeden, W. Taormina. Twelve Trees Press, 1986.

Williams, T. Memoirs. New Directions, 2006.

Taormina, one of the most beautiful cities in Sicily. It was called "a little patch of paradise" by Goethe.

Duomo Square, Taormina.

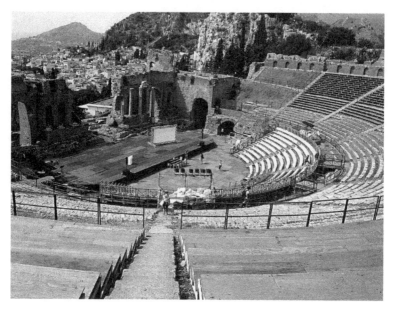

Taormina's Teatro Greco is arguably the most impressive of the surviving ancient Greek theaters.

Taormina's Casa Cuseni was a favorite refuge for Tennessee Williams and Henry Faulkner.

A medieval clock tower marked the entrance to the Jewish Quarter of Taormina.

Street sign in the old Jewish quarter in Taormina.

This municipal building with Jewish stars used to be a synagogue.

Duomo Square in Catania with the smiling Elephant obelisk in its center is designated as a World Heritage site.

CHAPTER 11: CATANIA, SICILY

The Medieval Castle
and the Menorah

The third largest city of Sicily, Catania lies in close proximity to the majestic mountain Etna. The city was always at the mercy of the brooding moods of that volcano. In the late 1600s, Etna struck twice, first drowning Catania and over 12,000 of its inhabitants in boiling lava, and then, in less than 25 years, leveling the city again with a murderous earthquake. Only 2,000 people survived. However, like Phoenix rising out of the ashes, Catania, rebuilt by architects from Rome, was reborn as one of the greatest baroque cities of the Mediterranean. Today, many tourists skip Catania hurrying instead to Taormina or Siracusa, and this was a mistake we were not going to make. For Jewish history pilgrims, Catania has a few unexpected gifts to offer.

Often overlooked by tourists, Catania is a masterpiece of Sicilian Baroque

Catania radiates romantic beauty with its broad boulevards, spacious squares, grandiose palazzos, and great cathedrals, striking in their black and white colors of lava and limestone, in spite of crumbling plaster and cracked marble columns.

Catania's main square with the Duomo Cathedral in its center is a World Heritage Site, and is dazzling in its majestically theatrical beauty. Here is Catania at its best, showcasing its black lava and white limestone baroque grandeur. In front of the Duomo is Fontana dell'Elephante, a funny black lava elephant that smiles at us while carrying a huge Egyptian obelisk on its back. Renowned composer Vincenzo Bellini, born and bred in Catania, is buried in the Duomo. His presence is felt everywhere: monuments, a house-museum, and even a beloved Sicilian dish, Pasta alla Norma, which is named after Bellini's world-famous opera. However, we learned that pasta was also homage to the volcano as well. Black olives represent lava, red tomatoes symbolize Etna's fire, and white cheese is supposed to look like the mountain snow.

Founded by the Greeks in the 8th century BC, Catania became the most prosperous Sicilian city during the Roman age, and still boasts not one but two Roman amphitheaters. The smaller one, near Piazza St. Francesco d'Assisi, was built, as the Romans often did, on top of a Greek theater. The larger one, the largest in Sicily, was a Roman original and could accommodate 16,000 spectators. Now we can admire parts of that great structure near Piazza Stesicoro.

If you are willing, Catania will unveil its treasures for you. One of them is a mystery embedded in the stone wall of a medieval castle.

Traces of the Jewish presence in the Emperor's castle

The majestic 13th-century Ursino Castello built by the Emperor Frederick II von Hohenstaufen, is the only city structure not destroyed by Etna during the 17th-century eruption and earthquake. The castle was designed to be the city's guardian, situated on the top of a seafront cliff. But the volcano changed the landscape, and the Castello is now landlocked. Inside the Castello is the city museum, Museo Civico, which contains, among other artifacts, a few Jewish funerary epitaphs.

In his book, *Between Scylla and Charybdis: The Jews in Sicily*, distinguished historian Shlomo Simonhson describes one of these epitaphs as evidence of the Jewish presence in Catania in the 4th century AD. That tombstone is dated 383 AD and is dedicated to Aurelieus Samuel and his wife Lasia Erine. The first line of the epitaph is in Hebrew and contains Samuel's name, followed by the evocation of peace onto Israel, which, as the author states, was customary at that time in the Diaspora. The rest is written in Latin and evokes the protection of the Lord and the Palestinian Patriarchs, the office that was abolished in the 5th century. It is interesting that though the husband's name is written in Hebrew, his wife's is only in Greek. As Simonhson notes that most Jewish epitaphs made during the 5th-8th centuries contained no Hebrew at all, which perhaps is a proof of the community being fully assimilated into the island's Greco-Roman culture of that period.

However, we found that the most interesting and undisputedly Jewish feature of the castle was outside. Right near the front gates, the castle's massive wall displays a menorah laid out in small black lava stones like a mosaic. Perhaps the Jews working on the construction wanted to write their own page in the city's history, still talking to us today, after many centuries of instilled forgetfulness.

Selected Sources

Scifo, A. Palazzo Biscari. Prestigious Baroque Architecture in Catania. Atma Publisher, 2006.

Simonhson, S. Between Scylla and Charybdis: The Jews in Sicily. Brill Books, 2011.

Catania Cathedral is a true masterpiece of Sicilian Baroque.

In spite of their crumbling plaster, Basilica Collegiata and other Catania churches are still striking.

Catania University.

Beautiful black lava and white limestone buildings in Catania
proudly display their former grandeur.

The majestic 13th-century Ursino Castello is the only city structure not destroyed by Etna during the 17th-century eruption.

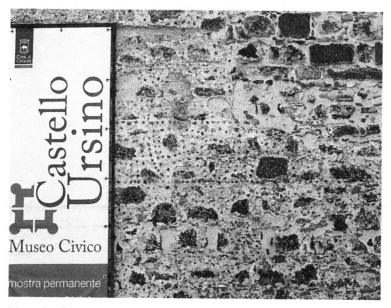

Near the front gates, it is possible to trace an image of a menorah laid out in small black lava stones like a mosaic.

View on Cagliari, the capital city of Sardinia, an island famed for its unearthly beauty.

Discovering Jewish Connections in Cagliari and Nora

Leaving Sicily, we continued our search of long-forgotten traces of Jewish history on another island - Sardinia.

A forty-minute Ryanair flight brought us to Sardinia, an island famed for its unearthly beauty. Sardinia is second only to Sicily in its size among the Mediterranean islands. Like Sicily, Sardinia attracted numerous waves of invaders: Phoenicians, Carthaginians, Romans, Byzantines, Arabs, the Italian city-states of Pisa and Genoa, and the Spanish Kingdom of Aragon—all succeeded one another in dominating the island. The Northern Italians came last, with Garibaldi himself falling in love with the island. He chose to live the last years of his life in Carpera, Sardinia.

Renowned for its great beaches and luxury resorts overflowing with tourists from all over the world, Sardinia tightly guards its ancient secrets, but for the persistent Jewish history pilgrims, these secrets reveal themselves, one story at a time.

The beginning of the Sardinian Jewish story

The first facts about the Jews in Sardinia came to us from Flavius Josephus, born Joseph ben Matityahu. This first-century Roman-Jewish scholar recorded in his study Antiquities that in 19 AD, four thousand Jews were deported to Sardinia from Rome by the Emperor Tiberius. Flavius noted with sadness that the emperor "punished so many" for the "crimes of the few." These "few" were four crooks who persuaded a senator's wife, a convert to Judaism, to invest large sums of money in a non-existent synagogue, which these liars claimed to represent. The Emperor hoped that the Jews would perish in Sardinia. Instead, the numerous descendants of the exiles built a prosperous life for themselves and became indispensable for the island's rulers in trade, finance, money-lending, crafts, and medicine. In the city of Alghero during the Aragonese (Spanish) rule, the Jews were exempt from paying customs duties and were even allowed to display the royal coat of arms on the synagogue as a sign of their importance to the Crown. While the island's largest Jewish community was in Alghero, thriving communities existed in a number of other Sardinian cities, like Sinai, Nora, and Cagliari, the island's capital.

As recorded in *Jewish Encyclopedia*, archeologists note that Sardinia is one of the few places in Italy with catacombs containing Jewish inscriptions written in "ebraico-latino" or Hebrew with Latin. Even today, the Sardinian language contains what linguists call "a hint at a Jewish presence," a few words that might represent an influential Jewish presence. For example, the word *caputanni* for September is a literal translation of Rosh Hashanah as "head of the year."

Walking through Jewish Cagliari

In Cagliari, our first stop was the Il Castello district of the island's capital. Named after the medieval hilltop castle, Il Castelo or Su Castedu in Sardinian is one of the most photographed iconic images of Cagliari. Built first by the Pizans and then by the Aragonese, this city within the city with its gothic and baroque palazzi of Italian and Spanish aristocrats was also a home to a prosperous Jewish community. Even today, 500 years after the expulsion and total annihilation of the Sardinian Jewry, the area of Il Castelo called Ghetto degli Ebrei is one of the most attractive places in Sardinia for Jewish history pilgrims. The former Jewish Ghetto is located north of the medieval Torre del'Elefante, built by the Pizans as a defensive structure against the Aragonese. In the late 1400s, all Cagliari Jews were forced to move into this small area located between the streets Via Santa Croce and Via Stretta and to wear special identifying clothes. In the years preceding the infamous Edict of Expulsion, the ominous influence of the "Most Catholic Monarchs," Ferdinand and Isabella of Spain, was painfully felt in Cagliari.

Walking though the winding narrow streets of Ghetto degli Ebrei, we found the Church of Santa Croce. During this trip we learned that in both Sicily and Sardinia, the churches' names like St. Giovanni

(John the Baptist) or Santa Croce (Holy Cross) served often as an indication that they were built on the foundation of a demolished or reconsecrated synagogue. As a 2006 restoration confirmed, Cagliari Santa Croce was indeed built using the main synagogue's structure. Only the neighborhood's name "Ghetto degli Ebrei" points at the historical Jewish presence, while the former military barracks built on the foundation of the old Jewish houses display the sign "Centro Comunale d'Arte e Cultura il Ghetto." But this is an exhibition place now, with no connection to Sardinian Jewish history.

Garbage dump on the site of a Jewish cemetery

Rabbi Barbara told me that the Cagliari Jewish community, though not the largest in Sardinia, created an important center of Jewish life in the island's capital. In the late 1990s, Rabbi Barbara's friend, a Sardinian engineer named Giacomo Sandri, helped to discover an early medieval Jewish site in Cagliari. The site represented a complex world centered on the synagogue with a mikveh and a garden for a sukkah around it. The entire archaeological site was soon covered up to make way for new construction, and today, a garbage dump covers the ancient Jewish cemetery. Discovered artifacts were sent to the Cagliari Museum. However, when we visited the museum in September 2014, none were on display; instead, the Jewish artifacts were kept in storage for preservation. One artifact that I was interested in was shipped, as the curator on duty explained, to the Metropolitan Museum of Art in New York City for their show "Assyria to Iberia at the Dawn of the Classical Age." It was the famous Nora Stone, the oldest existing example of the first alphabet, also called Proto-Canaanite or early Hebrew alphabet.

Little-known connections: the city of Nora and early Hebrews

Our next stop was the city of Nora situated on the south coast of Sardinia. Believed to be the first city founded in this island, Nora dates to the 11th century BC. This ancient city, most of which is said to be underwater, is of high interest to archaeologists. Nora was one of the most important centers of Phoenician expansion in the Mediterranean. Enterprising maritime traders, the Phoenicians were a

Semitic people who spoke a language similar to Hebrew and were the first group to colonize both Sicily and Sardinia, attracted by Sardinia's strategic location near important sea routes linking the Mediterranean with the Near East. The area was also rich with metal deposits, such as copper, iron, lead, and silver. The Phoenicians established their stronghold on the island; archaeological findings in Israel prove they imported silver during biblical times.

For me personally, Nora with its famous Nora Stone is placed forever at the roots of all recorded history and written literature of Western civilization. The Nora Stone, dating to the 9th century BC, was found at Nora in the late 1700s. The stone's incised writing is considered to be the first alphabet. Unlike cuneiform script, one of the earliest known systems of writing that relied on multiple pictorial symbols, the Nora alphabet used less than thirty letters, one for each sound, and was written like Hebrew, from right to left. This Phoenician invention—alphabetic writing—spread across the world they colonized. By the first millennium BC, the people of the Levant, including the Phoenicians and Arameans, or Hebrews, were using a standardized alphabet, which was soon transformed to create other written languages such as Greek, Etruscan, and Latin. The very word "alphabet" comes from "aleph" and "bet," the first two letters of the Phoenician writing system.

In Nora, not much is left from the Phoenicians. What visitors see today is mostly from the Roman period. The sunken city of Nora, as it is called, seems suspended between the sea and the sky, and walking through its ruins was almost a mythical experience. I could not help but think that, like the Phoenicians, who disappeared from history by being absorbed into much stronger civilizations of the Carthaginians and the Hebrews, the Jews of Sardinia were also pushed into historic oblivion, by forces of anti-Semitism and religious intolerance.

Jewish Sardinia today

Only a few Sardinian Jewish families returned to their ancestral island after the establishment of the unified state of Italy in the 1880s. Tragically, most of their descendants were killed during the Holocaust. Today there are very few Jews living in Sardinia, and there is no formal Jewish community on the island. However, just like in

Sicily, an increasing number of people who suspect that they have Jewish roots are rediscovering these roots through the study of Judaism. Giacomo Sandri, an engineer from Cagliari, who assisted in discovering the ancient Jewish site there, wrote a book on Sardinian Jewish history and made an Orthodox-style conversion to Judaism. Since 1992, Rabbi Barbara has been officiating at conversions of the Sardinian Anousim, descendants of those who were forced to give up their Jewish identity over 500 years ago.

Today, Sardinia seeks to demonstrate the island's resolve to remember its Jewish history and to preserve the evidence of Jewish civilization in Sardinia. On September 22, 2013, a square in Alghero was renamed *Plaça de la Juharia* (the Square of the Jews), recalling the fact that the square was once the center of the city's Jewish quarter and the place where the main synagogue was located. This event, which was attended by hundreds of people, opened with the song "Avinu Malkeinu" performed by a local band. Taking part in the inauguration were Alghero's mayor as well as the Israeli ambassador to Italy, who said: "This is a historic and symbolic gesture." The mayor then delivered a speech and said that he would like to rectify the injustice caused to the town's Jews in the past. He concluded by calling on Jews to return to Alghero. "Welcome home," he said (*Israel Jewish Scene*, September 30, 2013).

The Anousim: what we learned from the "Children of the Forced Ones" in Sicily and Sardinia

In the contemporary European context of increasing anti-Semitic and anti-Israeli attitudes sometimes escalating to violence, Sicily and Sardinia present a new and unusually optimistic chapter in the history of the Jewish Diaspora. Our own journey in search of Jewish stories on these two islands brought our understanding of both Jewish history and Jewish identity to a new level.

The destruction of synagogues and the burning of "Judaizers" five centuries ago failed to extinguish the Jewish spirit. Rabbi Barbara told numerous stories, some from her own family, of traditions whose meaning was often forgotten but that survived in their homes' secret cellars and in people's hearts. Cooking continued to conform to kosher dietary laws. Family burials were done outside the church with bodies rapped in simple shrouds. Special marriage blessings were recited in a "strange language" at home under a crocheted canopy. Deathbed confessions of Jewish ancestry to the families were common. The Anousim descendants, whose heritage was so cruelly stolen, hidden, and ignored, sustained their history in their flesh and blood. And perhaps it is the call of blood that drives a continuously growing number of B'nei Anousim to search for their historical legacy and reclaim it.

Most Anousim have no records to prove their Jewishness, they just know that this is who they are. Traditional Judaism does not recognize their claim. It took over twenty years for Conservative Judaism to pass a resolution recognizing the Anousim and creating a welcoming space for those who want to return to the Jewish people. In the early 1990s, Rabbi Barbara Aiello, the first reform Rabbi in Italy, became a leader of the southern Italian B'nei Anousim movement. For over 25 years, Rabbi Barbara has been performing numerous conversions, Bar Mitzvahs, and weddings, and organizing educational events for Jews and non-Jews alike. In Sicily and Sardinia, a Jewish cultural and religious renaissance is on the rise, with events centered on Jewish history taking a prominent place in the intellectual environment of the south of Italy.

While working on my Sicilian-Sardinian study, I came across Steven Spielberg's speech addressing the audience during the commemoration of the 70th anniversary of Auschwitz liberation. "If you are a Jew today," said the founder of the Shoah Foundation, "you know that we're once again facing the perennial demons of intolerance. Anti-Semites, radical extremists and religious fanatics that provoke hate crimes — these people want to, all over again, strip you of your past, of your story and of your identity … causing Jews to again leave Europe." (*World Jewry Digest*, January 2015). It seems, I thought, that southern Italy and especially my beloved Sicily, prove to be different, once again trying to recreate the once and future world of acceptance and multiculturalism. *Sheh Elohim Yevarech Othca*—may this be blessed.

Selected Sources

Dyson, S. Archeology and History in Sardinia from the Stone Age to Middle Ages: Shepherds, Sailors, and Conquerors. University of Pennsylvania Press, 2007.

Sorge, A. Legacy of Violence: History, Society, and the State in Sardinia. University of Toronto Press, 2015.

Torre del'Elefante in Il Castello district of Cagliari. The former Jewish Ghetto was located north of this medieval tower.

Via Santa Croce, the main street in Cagliari's Ghetto degli Ebrei (Jewish Ghetto).

The Church of Santa Croce was built on the site of the destroyed synagogue of Cagliari.

View of Nora, the first city in Cagliari built by the Phoenicians in the 11th century BC.

The Nora Stone (9th century BC) was found at Nora in the 1700s.
The Stone's incised writing is considered to be the first alphabet.

A giraffe in Serengeti National Park, Tanzania.

CHAPTER 13: AFRICA

Tracking Jewish Stories from the Streets of Nairobi to the Plains of Serengeti

Surprisingly for many of our friends, our trip to Africa was a very personal one for me. My late father, a secular intellectual with a strong Jewish identity, dreamt of Africa for the most of his life. Hating the dreary confining reality of Soviet Russia, my father imagined Africa as a mythical place where all God's creatures roam free. I knew that at some point in our lives, my quest for Jewish narratives around the globe would eventually bring us to Africa.

When we departed for Nairobi, our friends joked: "It will be a challenge to find your Jewish stories among the wildebeests!" "You'll see," I said. "I'll find a few good ones." So here they are.

Story number one: Africa as a personal journey

My father led me to Africa. This is how my first African Jewish story began, almost fifty years ago, in Soviet Russia.

I grew up surrounded by thousands of books collected by my parents over the years. And within this library, what I loved the most were my father's books about wild animals. For years, I slept with Kenneth Anderson's *The Black Panther of Sivanipalli* stuck under my pillow. Gerald Durrell's *My Family and Other Animals* was on my desk until I left for college. But my most favorite book was *Serengeti Shall Not Die* by Bernhard and Michael Grzimek. They were father and son, both biologists from Frankfurt, Germany. In the 1950s, the Grzimeks were the first scientists relentlessly working to preserve the Serengeti ecosystem, which they believed to be the last wonder of free nature in the world. I memorized the passages so often quoted by my father: "...in the coming decades, men will not travel to view marvels of engineering but they will leave the dusty towns in order to behold the last places on earth where God's creatures are peacefully living...Man-made structures can be rebuilt...but once the wild animals of the Serengeti are exterminated, no power on earth can bring them back..."

My husband and I arrived in Serengeti, Tanzania, decades after my father recited aloud the passages from the Grzimeks' book. We found their graves on the rim of the Ngorongoro Crater: Michael, whose plane crashed there in 1959 when he was a few months shy of his twenty-fifth birthday and Bernard, whose ashes were brought from Frankfurt in 1987 to rest next to his son.

Some time ago, while studying the German response to the Holocaust, I learned that Bernard Grzimek did something else in his life in addition to saving Serengeti. He had been saving Jewish lives for years during World War II, while risking his own life. He was a high-level official in the Nazi Food Ministry and managed to smuggle food for Jewish families in hiding. When the Gestapo suspected him, Grzimek fled underground.

As I told the Grzimeks' story to our friends who came with us to Africa, we could see zebras crossing the road, impalas grazing nearby, and baboons trying to figure out if we forgot to close the windows in our safari vehicle. Quoting the title of one of the Grzimek's books in my father's library, I said: "We are among animals of Africa, where all creatures roam free."

I placed two stones on the Grzimeks' grave. "Were they Jewish?" asked my friends. "No, I said. "But my father was."

Story number two: Kenya boasts a hundred-year shul

My second Jewish story of Africa began a few months before our departure, when out of the blue I Googled "synagogue in Kenya." My grandmother used to say: "We Jews are everywhere." And indeed we are. There it was, a beautiful synagogue building looking at me from the computer screen as if saying: "and why are you surprised, eh?"

I emailed the Synagogue and soon received a response from one of its leaders, Barbara Steenstrup. She later introduced me to Bunnie Gordon, who now lives in Maryland and serves as a Treasurer for the American Friends of Nairobi Hebrew Congregation. Both ladies told me their stories and explained what brought them to Kenya and how they found warmth and friendship among the Synagogue members which truly made Africa their new home. There, my new friends encountered a long-established and thriving Jewish community. In 2004, the Nairobi Hebrew Congregation celebrated its 100th birthday and in 2012, the centennial of its first building. The Nairobi Jewish community is as diverse as the Diaspora itself. Secular and observant, Sephardic and Ashkenazi, congregants come from India, Russia, Morocco, Poland, South Africa, and the United States. Some are native-born Kenyans, but most came from Israel. Some are from diplomatic corps; most are involved in various businesses.

The very first Jew arrived in Kenya in 1900 during the construction of the British railroad, a project managed from India. So the first Jewish merchant also arrived to Nairobi from British India. His name was Markus, a Romanian by origin, and he came to organize a supply of agricultural machinery for farmers who came from Europe. The Jewish population doubled the next year when Michael Hartz arrived to establish his tinsmith business in Nairobi. More followed later, some from Ukraine and Poland, others from Germany and Austria, and in 1904 the first congregation was established. The first Synagogue building was completed in December 1912.

Never numerous, Kenyan Jews, however, were remarkably influential in the development of the country. Farmers and doctors, businessmen and lawyers, they helped to bring Kenya into the 20th century, and in spite of the open anti-Semitism of the British settlers, the Jews of Nairobi heroically served the Empire through two world wars.

Anti-Semitism was rather obvious in Nairobi clubs and private schools: clubs did not accept Jews as members, and many private schools did not accept Jewish students. Public schools did, but gentile parents often would not allow their children to play with Jewish kids. Africa was not a safe haven from European Jew-hatred. The tide turned, however, during World War II, when the Nairobi congregation, closely working with the Jewish Refugee Committee in London, played a decisive role in saving countless European Jewish lives. The Board for Kenya Jewry, later named the Jewish Council for Training and Settlement, was charged with obtaining visas and looking after the refugees' welfare.

Vibrant Jewish life was stimulated by dozens of various organizations and societies created over some hundred-plus years in Nairobi, such as the Relief Fund for European Jewry, the Zionist Association, the Jewish Cultural Society, the Board for Jewish Education, and many others.

There are some devoted black followers of Judaism in Nairobi and it is known that there are hundreds of natives in Western Kenya who consider themselves Jewish. My grandmother would be proud.

Story number three: Masai warriors – "God's chosen people"

I found my third Jewish story of Africa in the most unlikely of places: the vast plains of the Masai Mara and Serengeti reserves. As we drove along bumpy and dusty roads, we saw the light-skinned, tall, and slender people dressed in red, who were as ubiquitous to the landscape as the sky above and the earth below. Surrounded by their herds of cattle, they leaned on their long spears or stood on one leg in a stork-like pose. Bearing remarkable similarities to the ancient Romans from North Africa, most had classical profiles, wore red togas and sandals, and wore Roman-style short stabbing swords. Women shaved their heads, while the young men's hair was plated and stuck together with red clay. To us, they looked like young mythical gods. These are the proud Masai (sometimes referred to as Maasai) people of East Africa, whose mysterious past is enveloped in legends of being one of the lost tribes of Israel.

When the Europeans brought the railroad to Nairobi, the Masai were the only human inhabitants there, coming and going as they pleased with their cattle. Nomadic and highly suspicious of any strangers passing through their land, the Masai were never fond of the Europeans. In 1904, M. Merker, a German official-turned scientist stationed in Tanganyika, learned the Maa language of the Masai, earned their trust (or thought he did), and collected the legends the Masai cared to share. In those legends of origin, the Masai, according to Merker, maintained that their ancestors were slaves in the land of the Nile and escaped through a parted sea, pursued by a vicious ruler. Long before the arrival of missionaries, Merker stated, the Masai knew the tales of Adam and Eve, and of Noah and the Great Flood, though under different names.

212

"I regard the Masai as being descended from the nomadic Semites to whom the oldest Hebrew pastoralist belong," pronounced Merker in his study. Lord Churchill called Merker's Dei Masai "the most truly inspired investigation that ever an African people has had." Merker's study was well-known to the British Colonial Secretary Sir Joseph Chamberlain, who in the early 1900s suggested to Theodore Herzl, the leader of the Zionist movement, that parts of "Masailand" could be handed over to persecuted Eastern European Jews. In the following hundred years, most researchers concluded that the Masai had Nilotic (from the river Nile) rather than Semitic, origins, but Merker's theory of the Masai as "one of the lost ten tribes of Israel" stubbornly continues to float in popular imagination.

We arranged to visit a Masai village to meet them. The villagers greeted us with singing and dancing, dressed in their best. Unlike other African tribes, the Masai refuse to modernize. They will not drive cars or wear western clothes. A couple of young men spoke enough English to communicate with us. When asked about their beliefs, they explained that the Masai believe in one God who they call Engai. Engai, they say, has two faces: the first face is black, kind and benevolent, bringing thunder and rain, grass for the cattle, and good life for the Masai. The second face is red and fearsome, bringing lighting and drought, famine and death. Engai made the Masai his chosen people and gave them the land of Africa.

The word "Masai" is synonymous with "cattle," these young people said. They translated a traditional greeting: "How are your wives and children and how is your cattle?" To own one without the other means to be poor; to have an abundance of both is to be rich. Cattle do not just give meaning to Masai life, they are life.

As we went around the village, we were told of the traditions curiously resembling those of the Jews: the Masai would never eat meat the same day they drink milk; they consider that to be highly unhealthy to both people and cattle.

The Masai do not have chiefs. Instead, their lives are governed by a collective of elders chosen for their wisdom and moral qualities. Their assembly is called Sanhedrin and the round hut where they get together is called a Tabernacle. When a highly respected elder dies, he is buried in the ground facing east. Every passer-by places a stone on the grave as a sign of respect, and after a while, a small hill appears above the grave.

All the Masai wear bright jewelry with colors symbolizing the Masai universe: red stands for blood of a slaughtered animal; white symbolizes milk that sustains the Masai; orange stands for milk mixed with blood, a drink that the Masai like and believe to provide strength and nourishment; green is the color of the grass that feeds their cattle; and the blue is the sky above the Masai land given by Engai to his chosen people.

Story number four: home away from home in Nairobi

I collected my fourth Jewish story in Africa at the end of our trip. We were traveling all day through the exotic strangeness of the Zanzibar Stone Town to the Nairobi airport's thick mess of people and suitcases, sickening smells, and deafening noises. Through the traffic and dust and darkness of the Nairobi streets, like a mirage in the wilderness, we saw a brilliantly-lit Jewish star. "Are you meeting with Barbara?" a voice asked. We were.

Barbara Steenstrup, beautiful and smiling, was waiting for us on the steps of the Nairobi Hebrew Congregation synagogue. It was too dark to see the garden surrounding the building but we could smell it. The aroma felt almost divine. For the first time that day, we deeply inhaled and smiled back.

Barbara gave us a detailed tour. I had read the book she sent me about the history of the congregation and I studied the synagogue's website. But to step into that beautiful building in real life was entirely different. There was something in the main sanctuary's colors of warm wood, bright blue, and gold that warmed my heart. I could not believe that we were standing in the shul, right in the heart of African darkness, but it felt so familiar at the same time.

Barbara treated us to a delicious fruit cake and coffee. We met the synagogue's facility manager, a delightful Kenyan, Aggrey Muchene. Two travelers from Cleveland, Ohio, a Kenyan from a neighboring village, and a lady from Baltimore—we talked about the difficult life in Kenya and our families, the recent devastating fire at the Nairobi airport and this beautiful synagogue.

I thought about the meaning of a Jewish identity: expansive and inclusive, it may stretch much beyond what we think of as Ashkenazi or Sephardic. What is the Jewish Diaspora? I asked myself. Could it be simply defined as a removal from one's homeland? There is something in us, Jews, I thought, a truly eternal people that moves us, no matter where we are, to always create a space of cultural solidarity and expression of community.

A home away from home. Even when we are in Africa.

Selected Sources

Grzimek, B., Grzimek, M. Serengeti Shall Not Die. Ballantine Books, 1973.

Hull, R. Jews and Judaism in African History. Marcus Wiener Publishers, 2009.

Saitoti, T. O. The World of a Maasai Warrior. University of California Press, 1988.

Salvatori, C. Glimpses of the Jews of Kenya: The Centennial Story of the Nairobi Hebrew Congregation, 1904-2004. Nairobi Hebrew Congregation, 2004.

The Grzimeks' grave on the rim of the Ngorongoro Crater, Tanzania. Both scientists dedicated their lives to the animals of Africa.

A Masai tribe greeting procession welcomes us at the entrance to their village, Kenya.

Masai warriors engage in their traditional dance competition, Kenya.

Masai wife near her hut. Masai women shave their heads after marriage.

Masai Healer in his village, Kenya.

Brightly-lit Star of David at the entrance to the Nairobi Synagogue, Kenya.

Nairobi Hebrew Congregation Synagogue.

Inside the sanctuary of the Nairobi Synagogue.

The author and photographer with the Vice President of the Nairobi Synagogue, Barbara Steenstrup, Kenya.

The Pit (yama) Memorial in Minsk. Courtesy of Alla Abrukin.

CHAPTER 14: THE SOVIET UNION

Our Narratives, Ourselves

"No monument stands over Babi Yar. A drop sheer as a crude gravestone. I am afraid. Today I am as old in years as all the Jewish people." Yevgeny Yevtushenko, 1961.

I did not travel anywhere to find this story. It lives within me, as it does within most Jewish people's hearts and minds. These are our personal Holocaust narratives: pain and loss, lives interrupted, generations unborn, and post-war silence and indifference. Multitudes of these internalized narratives are recorded, but many are still untold.

The Soviet Union and my family's Holocaust narrative

I grew up knowing Yevtushenko's poem by heart. He wrote it to expose the incomprehensible inhumanity of Babi Yar, a place in Kiev where the Nazis massacred the entire Jewish population. My grandmother Sonia's family from Vileyka was similarly murdered, along with all the Jews of that small town during the German occupation. In the early 1920s, when Sonja left Vileyka to follow her Communist-scientist husband Michael Kopeliovich to the Soviet Ukraine, Vileyka was in Poland. Stalin's purges followed, when Michael, a Deputy Minister of Education, was arrested and soon executed by the NKVD (predecessor of the KGB). Meanwhile, Sonia hid to avoid being arrested herself. My grandmother did not find out about her Polish family's fate until well after World War II. By that time, Vileyka, annexed by the Soviet Union, became part of the Soviet republic of Belarus. Until the breakup of the Soviet Union, neither the Polish nor Soviet government ever recognized what happened during World War II to the European Jewry in general and to their own Jewish citizens in particular.

Even though the word "Holocaust" came into widespread usage at the end of the 1960s, it was only when I arrived in the U.S. in 1982 that I learned about the Nazi "Final Solution" and heard the word for the first time. Communist governments had their specific methods for controlling historic memory both within the Soviet republics and in the Soviet Bloc countries. According to a 2012 study published in the *Geschichtswerkstatt Europa*, in Belarus, like elsewhere in the Soviet Union, the government completely rejected any notion of national identity. The official propaganda talked about the number of Soviet people killed by the enemy during the war but never mentioned the atrocities committed against the Jews as part of the Nazi extermination program. The very word "Jewish" was never used and instead, vague "Soviet patriotic citizens" were commemorated. In Poland, on the contrary, nationality—Polish, to be specific—was paramount for the Party. Stalin ordered his satellite country to build a stable ethnic society. In addition to the prevailing anti-Semitic attitudes of Polish citizens who did not want their surviving Jewish compatriots to return from the camps, the Polish government saw the Holocaust remembrance as a reminder of multinational Poland, and therefore disagreeable with the official policy. The Soviets suppressed any hint of the Nazi "Final Solution" for the same reason they covered up other wartime crimes, such as the massive collaboration with the Nazis in the Soviet territory and in the countries that would become members of the Soviet Bloc. The Soviet government's goal was to conceal the Nazis' mass killing of the Jews, while blaming the Germans for their own atrocities like the Katyn Massacre when the Red Army executed more than twenty thousand Polish officers in the Katyn forest. The regime did not want questions about its own strategies of ethnic relocations, mass purges, and concentration camps. These strategies were learned well by the Nazis when they implemented their own genocide programs.

So, in my family, we read Yevtushenko's poem as an indictment of the Soviets' official refusal to acknowledge the Holocaust.

Vileyka revisited

In October 2014, Hanoch Ben-Yami, my Israeli cousin and dear friend, who is currently the head of the Philosophy Department at the Central European University in Budapest, decided to visit Vileyka while giving a series of talks at the Belarusian State University in Minsk. Hanoch's mother, Ruth Ben-Yami, was born in Vileyka. Hanoch's grandmother, Haya, traveled to Poland from Paris to give birth to her first child in her parents' house. Haya and Sonya, Hanoch's and my grandmother, were sisters.

My cousin is the first of our post-war family ever to visit Vileyka. Hanoch called his visit "quite authoritative" because his guide was the director of the local museum. The house where his and my great-grandparents lived was burned down long ago, but the street still exists, though under a different name. As the museum director explained to Hanoch, only a few old houses remain in Vileyka and even fewer among them are known to have belonged to pre-war Jews. The small town looked dull and unkempt. "Nothing there," wrote Hanoch "commemorates the thriving Jewish community of the past."

Hanoch drove to the Jewish cemetery located outside the town. He described to me the rusty gate to the graveyard that was hanging on the stone wall covered with patches of old plaster here and there. There was a small memorial to those murdered in the war. It was erected, he was told, in the 1980s. The wording was in Hebrew, Yiddish, and English. Most Jews were murdered outside the town, but the memorial was placed in the cemetery, perhaps to make it easier to find.

Hanoch tried to find the graves of our family members buried before the war, but there were only a few tombstones left in the entire cemetery. There is no one in Vileyka that takes care of the Jewish cemetery. The locals took the tombstones to use as building material or grinding stones, or to pave town streets. The raised graves, however, had walls made from a mixture of gravel and cement, and could not be used for much, Hanoch described, so they are still there, although many are broken, perhaps just from neglect. All the inscriptions were on the stolen tombstones, wrote my cousin, so "the dead are lying there now in total anonymity." No one will know the exact location of the graves of our family members.

What we do know with some certainty is that in the 1920s and 1930s there were more Jews in Vileyka than Christians. Most were thriving, cultural, and assimilated like our great-grandfather, businessman Moshe Swirsky. Though agnostic and non-observant, he donated a lot of money to build the new synagogue and was one of the synagogue's last presidents. Knowing that the war was imminent, Moshe Swirsky refused to leave his hometown. According to my grandmother Sonia, he thought he knew the Germans well from his and Sonia's mother Miriam's frequent visits to Baden-Baden and his business dealings, and considered them to be a highly cultural nation. A much preferred choice, Swirsky thought, compared to the Soviets. Both our great-grandparents were alive when the Nazis invaded. That summer of 1941, they were joined by their two daughters, our grandmothers' younger sisters, Betya and Fanya. The sisters came from Tel-Aviv with their little children for a relaxed summer vacation. All of them were brutally murdered by the Nazis.

As documented by the descendants in the book Jewish Community of Vileyka published in Israel years after the war, the annihilation of the Jews of Vileyka was meticulously planned and executed in three "actions." The first victims were those reported by eager neighbors as Communists. They were shot in the woods of Malouny. In the second action, men, women, and children were dragged out of their houses and massacred in the place called Mayak (near Krivaya Sloboda). Their bodies were thrown into a common grave prepared in advance. The remaining Jews of Vileyka and surrounding villages were executed in the courtyard of the town prison, their corpses thrown into a deep pit and burned. This is how Jewish Vileyka was wiped from the face of the earth. The Swirsky family was probably murdered during the second action, but there is no way of knowing for sure. In our family's Holocaust narrative, we do not have a survivor story. My friend Raya does.

Raya narrates an untold survivor story

My friend of over 30 years is vivacious, funny, and beautiful. Raya is a highly positive person, optimistic and strong, a real pillar of support to her family and friends. She mentioned her mother's war-time story while we were visiting an unfinished Holocaust memorial in Milan, Italy. Over a year had passed, when, while working on this essay for my upcoming book, I asked Raya for a detailed recorded interview. She agreed, and this was the first time I heard my friend's voice trembling.

Raya's mother, Masha Rozenhous, was born in 1919 in Smolevichi, a small town in Belarus, some 22 miles east of the republic's capital Minsk and about 60 miles from my family in Vileyka. When Masha was still a strong woman of 65, she was killed by a drunk driver. Her husband Yakov Weinstein witnessed in horror when it happened. At that time, the family lived in Minsk. Raya was 27 years old then, already a young mother herself. She remembered how shocked she was when during the funeral her father kept repeating through tears: "You survived through so much horror, Mashen'ka, awful horror...and to get killed like that by a stupid car..." Yakov was a decorated war hero, who served in the Soviet Army all five years during the war and went as far as Berlin. "He fought through the entire war, lived through blood and death around him," Raya continued. "What horror that Mom had to go through was he talking about?" Raya also recalled her Mom's best friend, Lisa, a librarian at the Minsk Public Library, saying at the funeral: "Masha was the only one who survived Smolevichi ghetto." Ghetto? What?

Masha never talked about her life during the war, and it was Yakov who told Raya about the terrible events in her mother's life. I did some research on the Yad Vashem database and, with available English-language documents, filled in a few historical gaps. Somehow, I found more factual testimonies about what happened in Smolevichi than I was able to uncover about Vileyka.

The Germans occupied Smolevichi on June 26, 1941. Immediately, they established a ghetto, gathering all the local Jews, about 2,000 people. Some documents I read pointed out that the Smolevichi ghetto was among the first established by the Nazis in the Soviet territory. Liquidation operations began almost immediately. All of Smolevichi's Jews were murdered in a number of "actions" carried out by the Germans who were enthusiastically assisted by the local population between July 1941 and October 1942.

In early June 1941, Masha, who was a history major at the university, came home to spend the summer with her family. So did her younger brother Boris, a student at the Conservatory of Music. Their older sister Ida arrived from Moscow with her little child. The two oldest siblings, a brother and another sister, stayed in Moscow where they lived with their families. The mother, Rahil, managed a dry goods store. The father, according to Raya, was an intellectual and humanist educated as a Rabbi before the Bolsheviks took over in 1917. He passed away in 1940. By the end of June 1941, the Rozenhous family of Smolevichi, along with other local Jews, was forced into the ghetto.

On August 24 (Yakov told Raya that her mother thought it could be the first days of September) 1,300 to 2,000 Jews from Smolevichi, mostly old people, women, and children, were ordered to march toward Gorodishche-Kaplitsa Hill, a few miles south of town. Some people tried to resist, realizing that they were being herded to their execution. They were shot on the spot. The rest were brought to the site where they were forced to undress. They were then shot and thrown into the pit. Small children were thrown into that pit and buried alive. The murder operation was carried out by the Teilkommando [sub-unit] number 2 of the Einsatzkommando 8b, under the command of Werner Schoeneman, with the eager cooperation of the local police force (according to other sources, the murders were also carried out by two either Lithuanian or Belarusian units). Also present was local Police Battalion 707/10. Then, 250 more Jews (according to other data some 1,000 Jews) were similarly massacred on September 13, 1941. This murder was carried out under the command of the town's officer Mueller.

Raya did not know all the details I compiled from the Yad Vashem documents. Her father most probably did not know either. What Yakov revealed to Raya were a few crucial facts his wife shared with him, one heartbreaking story at a time.

Story number one: Feelings disappear. During the first few weeks in the overcrowded ghetto, Smolevichi villagers found the way to contact their former neighbors. "Give me your stuff (fur coat, couch, etc.)," they demanded. "You will be shot anyway." Masha thought that people in the ghetto, herself included, were losing their normal ability to feel. She remembered being constantly hungry, but not feeling shocked or disgusted or scared. It seemed no one cared about anything. Everyone was just trying to get through the day, one hour at a time.

Story number two: An open gate. On the day of the forced march to execution, Masha walked with her family along with the others. Passing by one house, she noticed an open gate leading to a small yard. She ran through the gate and hid. Masha was able to sneak away because an officer from their convoy was distracted: he was beating up an old woman who fell to the ground, unable to walk. So, Masha ran without thinking, without feeling. It seemed that her feet acted independently of her mind and carried her there. She waited till dark, and heard everything that was taking place at the Gorodishche-Kaplitsa Hill. Then, when all became quiet, she got out and walked.

Story number three: A long walk to survival. Masha wanted to get to a suburb of Minsk to find her non-Jewish friend Lisa (a librarian that Raya remembered at her mother's funeral). Tall, blond and blue-eyed, Masha walked over 22 miles, through German and local police checkpoints, without being stopped. Masha knew German well and sometimes she felt bold enough to ask for directions. She recalled experiencing no fear and feeling nothing. Just an impulse to walk. Raya remembered one piece of information that her mother did share with her, almost like a joke: "I could speak satisfactory German during the war but had to watch not to slip into Yiddish!" Masha found her friend and stayed a short time with the family. She had to leave soon though because her friend's family feared that Masha could be recognized by someone who knew her from the university. She left Lisa and walked from Minsk to Orsha, another large Belarusian city. Orsha is 136 miles from Minsk. Raya never found out how Masha got there and how long it took her.

In Orsha, Masha stayed for a while with an old woman, someone Lisa's family knew. Everyone there thought that she was Belarusian by nationality. As I learned from the BLJews Database, Orsha had over 25,000 Jews; the ghetto was established at the end of July 1941. In September of 1941 when Masha stayed in Orsha, the ghetto was not yet liquidated. Undoubtedly, Masha knew about the ghetto. She also knew well how the ghetto would end. The old woman boarded a few German officers. Something compelled Masha to start a conversation with them, and against any reasons of self-preservation, she asked them about the Jews, trying to sound like a Jew-hater. One officer kept his eyes on her for a long time, and then said: "Not every German is a murderer and thinks that Jews have to be annihilated."

Story number four: Working in Germany. The old Orsha woman had finally told Masha to *tikat* (Belarusian for "run"). She probably guessed who Masha really was. With other young Belarusian, Lithuanian, and Polish girls, Masha signed up to "voluntarily" go and work in Germany. She was assigned to work on a farm. There the girls were decently treated. They had to work hard, but so did the farmer's family. They slept in a barn and were not hungry. Just like the farmers, they ate boiled potatoes and sauerkraut. "Only the Russians would use uncooked cabbage," the farmers used to say, "like pigs." There also, the blond blue-eyed Masha passed herself for a Belarusian girl. She had nothing bad to say about the farmers. The young Polish women who worked on the same farm and slept in the same barn were the ones who treated her cruelly by ridiculing and ostracizing her. These Polish girls made Masha's life close to unbearable. They sensed something, Masha thought many years later. They called her *zhidivka* (a kike) and gleefully promised her total extermination of her "race." These women would not earn themselves better food or more comfortable accommodations by treating Masha with brutality. They simply were aggressively anti-Semitic.

Yakov told Raya that the only strong emotion Masha recalled experiencing during the war years was hatred. She hated the Germans but most of all she hated the Belarusians and the Poles. The former were the invaders, the ultimate enemy who organized extermination of the Jews; the latter, often former neighbors, were the enforcers, the most cruel torturers and murderers. Raya later remembered what she called her mother's "almost pathological hatred" toward the Poles.

Story number five: the Liberation. The part of Germany where Masha worked on the farm was captured by the Americans. She could have easily chosen to go to the U.S. but decided to return to Russia and find her surviving siblings in Moscow, the only loved ones she had left. She stayed in Moscow for a short time and returned back to Minsk in Belarus. "I never liked Moscow," she used to explain. Raya did not want to speculate on her reasons, but I thought of at least two. Masha's siblings could have unconsciously caused her to feel survivor's guilt: after all, she was the one left alive when the rest of the Smolevichi family was slaughtered. In addition, she could have been easily found out and arrested in Moscow as a "traitor," the fate of most Soviet returning POWs and those forced into slave labor in Germany.

Raya recalled that her mother had strange moments, when she would suddenly "disappear" into herself: with her face frozen and eyes blank, she seemed to listen to something inside her own mind. These episodes might happen when she walked along the street with her children. She would stop right in the middle of the crowd and turn around with a strange expression, as if fearing somebody lurking behind her back. Perhaps she saw or imagined something that triggered her disappearance into the depth of her mind or into her past.

When Raya paused, I asked her: "Did Rahil, Masha's mother, notice the gate first? Was Masha pushed there by her mother?" Raya said: "I don't know. And I don't want to guess. Mom just ran there and hid." I felt deeply ashamed for even asking this question, which suggested an easier accepted situation, and passing, alas unconsciously, judgment. The Holocaust defies understanding. And who are we, going through our lives in safety and comfort, to judge any victim of the Holocaust? Would Masha's story be "prettier" if she died along with her mother, brother, sister, and sister's child thrown alive into the pit? Then my friend Raya, her beautiful daughter Julia, and the funny, always smiling, one-year-old grandbaby Benjamin would never have been born. Sometimes it takes tremendous courage to choose life. Masha had that courage.

Soon after the war, Jews from different locations in the Soviet Union erected a monument at the Jewish cemetery of Smolevichi to commemorate their relatives and friends. The monument carries an inscription in Russian that reads: "To the memory of our loved ones murdered by the German invaders..." As was the sign of the times, no Jewish connections were allowed to be mentioned. Many years later, on June 26, 2000, a memorial stone was placed at the site where the Jews of Smolevichi were massacred. The stone was funded through a donation made by the Lazarus family of England.

The Pit (Yama) in Minsk

When Masha returned to Minsk, I am sure she heard about the fate of the local Jews. According to The Columbia Guide to the Holocaust, the Minsk ghetto was the largest ghetto the Nazis established in the occupied Soviet territories. Between 80,000 to 100,000 Jews of Minsk and the vicinity were forced into that ghetto; most were murdered. In 1947, a modest obelisk was erected near the place where thousands of Minsk Jews were massacred. The Minsk memorial is considered to be the first Soviet memorial dedicated to the Jewish victims of Nazism. For many years, it was also the only one that dared to proclaim openly in Yiddish: "Dedicated to the Jews, victims of Nazism."

At the end of the 1940s-early 1950s, during Stalin's anti-Semitic campaign against "cosmopolitism," both the poet Chaim Maltinski, who wrote a verse in remembrance of the murdered Jews, and the stonemason Morduch Sprishen, who chiseled these words on the obelisk, were arrested and sent to the Gulag for their "bourgeois and nationalistic" tendencies.

Hundreds of people attended the dedication ceremony. We do not know if Masha did. We also do not know what she thought about the memorial.

In 2000, long after Masha's death, a sculptured group was added to the old obelisk. The added group was created by Jewish Belarus architect Leonid Levin and Israeli sculptors Else Pollack and Alexander Finski. The entire complex is now called The Pit (*yama* in Russian). Placed at the site where Minsk Jews were killed, the monument is indeed a deep pit with a long granite staircase leading to the bottom.

A bronze group of twenty seven emaciated naked human figures descend along the steps toward their violent death. A violinist, pregnant woman, and children are among the group. Faces are not detailed, they just have an overall expression of horror.

It took eight years to complete the addition to the monument. All work was done by hand. The memorial, which I believe to be one of the best visual expressions of many families' Holocaust narratives, is a target of repeated vandalism.

Perhaps some things never change: there will always be those who are bent on destruction and those who are inspired to create. Let our families' Holocaust narratives, oral, written, or cast in bronze, be the creative force that preserves memories and builds bridges between the horrific past and the future in which inhuman atrocities should not be repeated. May we always choose life.

L'Chaim.

Selected Sources

Dunets, N., Kostrzewa, K., Binkin, G. "Official Soviet Attitude towards the Holocaust in Homel and Wolomin. Transnational Analysis of the Holocaust Remembrance," Geschichtswerkstatt Europa, April 2012.

Niewyk, D. L., Nicosia, F. R. The Columbia Guide to the Holocaust. Columbia University Press, 2003.

Yad Vashem Database: The Murder Sites of the Jews in the Occupied Territories of the Former U.S.S.R. http://www.yadvashem.org/untoldstories/database/index.asp?cid=552.

Belorussian Jews (BLJews) Database. http://www.beljews.info/Orsha.htm.

The memorial at the Jewish cemetery in Vileyka was erected in the 1980s. Courtesy of Hanoch Ben-Yami.

Vandalized Jewish cemetery in Vileyka. The locals took the tombstones and used them as building material. Courtesy of Hanoch Ben-Yami.

The first Holocaust memorial erected in the Soviet Union was in Minsk. Courtesy of the United States Holocaust Memorial Museum.

Dedication of the Holocaust memorial obelisk in Minsk in 1947. Courtesy of the United States Holocaust Memorial Museum.

The Pit (yama) Memorial in Minsk. Courtesy of Alla Abrukin.

ABOUT THE AUTHOR

An internationally-published art and travel writer, educator, and lecturer, Irene Shaland emigrated from St. Petersburg, Russia, to Cleveland, Ohio, with her husband Alex in 1982. Her first book *Tennessee Williams on the Soviet Stage* (University Press of America) had appeared in 1987, followed by *American Theater and Drama Research, 1945-1990*, (McFarland) in 1991. Irene's theater reviews were published in *American Theater, Theater Journal, Cleveland Plain Dealer* and *Cleveland Jewish News*. In addition to theater and the arts, Irene has a life-long passion for travel, and together with her husband Alex, photographer and travel partner, they visited over 60 countries. Irene's current book is the result of years of travel, research, and meetings and conversations with people in all parts of the globe. Her numerous articles dedicated to cultural and historical travel have appeared in magazines in the U.S., Canada, Kenya and the U.K. Irene holds a BA in Theater Journalism and Art History from St. Petersburg University (Russia), a Master's Degree in English from Case Western Reserve University (Cleveland, Ohio), and a Master's Degree in Information Sciences from Kent State University (Kent, Ohio). Irene and Alex reside in Lyndhurst, Ohio.

Website: http://globaltravelauthors.com
Twitter: @ShalandGTA
Facebook: https://www.facebook.com/GlobalTravelAuthors

About the Photographer

Alex Shaland is an internationally-published photographer. Alex's photographs appeared in various journals and other media in the U.S., Canada, France, Kenya, South Korea, and the U.K.